# ADDICTION

# ADDICTION

*How We Get Stuck and Unstuck
in Compulsive Patterns and Behavior*

## ROBERT P. VANDE KAPPELLE

WIPF & STOCK · Eugene, Oregon

ADDICTION
How We Get Stuck and Unstuck in Compulsive Patterns and Behavior

Wipf & Stock
An Imprint of Wipf and Stock Publishers
199 W. 8th Ave., Suite 3
Eugene, OR 97401

www.wipfandstock.com

PAPERBACK ISBN: 978-1-5326-9020-4
HARDCOVER ISBN: 978-1-5326-9021-1
EBOOK ISBN: 978-1-5326-9022-8

Manufactured in the U.S.A.                    MAY 16, 2019

To Georgia Lee Metsger, Jim Metsger,
Marybeth Duffy, and Jess Costa
Faithful warriors, wise guides, and loyal friends,
you make the invisible church visible.

God, give us grace to accept with serenity
the things that cannot be changed,
courage to change the things which should be changed,
and the Wisdom to distinguish the one from the other.

—REINHOLD NIEBUHR


God grant me the serenity
to accept the things I cannot change,
the courage to change the things I can,
and the wisdom to know the difference.

—SERENITY PRAYER

# Contents

# Preface

ADDICTION IS INCREASING, NOT decreasing, in society. Indeed, today, more people than ever before see themselves as addicted or recovering from substance addiction. In a national survey conducted in 2012, one in ten American adults—more than twenty-three million people—said they had kicked some type of drug or alcohol addiction in their lifetime. Added to this number, at least another twenty-three million adults currently suffer from some type of substance use disorder.[1] That doesn't include the millions who consider themselves addicted to or recovering from behaviors like sex, gambling, or online activities, not does it include food-related disorders. And the problem is not subsiding or going away.

While Big Pharma, Big Food, Big Tobacco, Big Alcohol, and Big Business all understand addiction and how to manipulate it, Big Government and most of the American public do not. As this book demonstrates, addiction is not a sin or a disease, as many commonly suppose. Even if addiction were a sin or disease, why, then, treat nonviolent addictions as crimes? Trapped in outdated ideas, our society continues to participate in hopeless debates while enforcing counterproductive criminalization strategies. We need to do better than that, far better.

People with addictions often say that the first step to recovery is hitting bottom. Unless there are trapdoors or subbasements, hitting bottom presents addicted individuals with two options: to remain at the bottom, or to pursue the grace inherent in turning upward. Why humans are addicted and how addictions are overcome are vitally important concerns. They will drive our study, and the answers will surprise you.

Speaking biologically, we are all addicted. That's how we are hard wired. As this book demonstrates, addiction is a pattern of learned behavior

1. Szalavitz, *Unbroken Brain*, 2.

that utilizes ancient mental pathways designed to promote survival and reproduction. Since those are the fundamental tasks of all biological organisms, brain patterns produce highly motivated behavior. When neural connections intended to promote eating, reproduction, parenting, and social relationships are diverted into addiction, their blessings can become curses.

When we humans are faced with a task, we can respond in one of three ways: we can avoid the experience, we can be overwhelmed by it, or we can confront it. While each response can produce addictive behavior, depending on temperament and experience, the third is the best candidate, at least for most human beings. For example, when I decide to write a book, I know that the task will require a commitment of time and energy lasting one or more years. In my case, engagement with a book project requires not only whole-hearted commitment but also top priority, meaning that the project will influence all my activities and relationships. To complete book projects successfully requires determination bordering on obsession. During my academic career, while teaching and helping to raise two active children, I wrote only sporadically, mostly at night, on weekends, and during the summer. However, now that I am retired, I have more time to read and write, and I do so compulsively. Twelve of my nineteen books have been written or completed in the past five years.

Work and writing are my obsession. What are your obsessions? Do you view your addictions positively, as ways to accomplish goals and dreams, or negatively, as misguided behavior that consumes your attention, diminishes your vitality, hinders your relationships, and distorts your self-image? It is this latter phenomena—the nature, causes, symptoms, consequences, and recovery from negative addictions—that we address in this study.

Ultimately, however, this book is not simply about addiction, but about what it means to be human, what it means to be you and me. By "you" I don't mean just the addictive you, but all of you. And by "all of you" I don't mean just you or me but all of us, people with severe addictions and people without such addictions. For the study of addiction is essentially an investigation of identity. An underlying theme in the chapters ahead is that the route to recovery does not depend simply on biology or psychology, but on spirituality and awareness, which require the mutual engagement of all members of society, addicted and non-addicted alike. This kind of mutual engagement can only take place when we recover a sense of shared identity. Elucidating this identity is an objective of this book.

# Disclaimer

The information in this book will not end poor parenting or the scourge of child abuse, poverty, racism, sexual discrimination, or obsessive consumerism, all contributors to today's addictive climate. Nor will it end alcoholism or eliminate drug addiction, the current opioid "epidemic,"[2] or personality disorders. However, if it makes readers less possessive, less obsessive in their everyday behavior, more generous, and better and wiser parents, grandparents, neighbors, and citizens, then it will have achieved its intention.

This material is intended for personal development and instructional use only, and is not appropriate for self-diagnosis. The author does not endorse a particular psychological methodology or spiritual approach to behavior therapy. Readers who believe they need professional help are encouraged to seek the assistance of a qualified therapist.

# Acknowledgments

This book is practical, not technical in nature; hence the paucity of footnotes. The perspective is inspired by journalist Maia Szalavitz's groundbreaking memoir, *Unbroken Brain*, and the influence of her account is evident throughout my text, particularly in segments regarding the nature of addiction, the behavioral traits associated with addictive patterns, the relationship of addiction to trauma and love, harm reduction, and neurodiversity (see chapters 1, 2, 4, 5, 6, 9, 11, and epilogue). On the sources of addictive behavior, including biological, psychological, and social aspects (see chapters 4, 8, and 9), I rely on clinical psychologist Jefferson Singer's insights and concepts found in *Message in a Bottle*, based on his interaction with chronically addicted men at a treatment center in Connecticut. Information on the neurological nature of addiction and on the role of love and spirituality in the healing of addiction (see chapters 2 and 10) is adapted from psychiatrist Gerald May's 1991 volume *Addiction and Grace*. The segment on materialism and consumerism (see chapter 7) is based on original research conducted by psychology professor Tim Kasser, narrated in his 2002 volume *The High Price of Materialism*. On the topic of spirituality and self-awareness (see chapter 8), I am indebted to lectures and works by Deepak Chopra, particularly his televised talk "The Seven Spiritual Laws

2. Representing 4.4 percent of the world's population, Americans consume roughly 30 percent of its opioids; International Narcotics Board data, cited in May, *Dopesick*, 186.

of Success." Finally, insights on the Enneagram, particularly as it relates to personality type, spirituality, and addiction (see chapter 12), come from Ron Riso and Russ Hudson, as described in works such as *Discovering Your Personality Type* (1995), *Personality Types* (1996), and *Understanding the Enneagram* (2000).

As always, I am indebted to my wife, Susan, a Gestalt Pastoral Care therapist, whose devotion at home and in the community enables and informs my writing. Her dedication to people at risk as well as to our own children and grandchildren exemplifies commitment to the present as well as the future, confirming the transformative power of generosity, compassion, and love.

# THE PROBLEM:

## ADDICTION

# CHAPTER 1

# The Nature of Addiction

Addiction is a learning disorder, a pattern of learned behavior.
—MAIA SZALAVITZ

ADDICTION AND DEPENDENCE, LIKE democracy and tyranny, are value-laden concepts, and in normal usage, they generally have a negative connotation. When we speak of addictive or compulsive behavior, what do we mean? Is dependence on a drug or on a pattern of behavior necessarily bad or harmful?

In every society, ordinary people frequently become dependent upon a variety of substances such as nicotine, caffeine, sugar, and chocolate. Some people, of course, become hooked on more harmful drugs. Is such reliance physical addiction, psychological dependence, or simply preference? In the past, experts argued that people could develop psychological dependence by habitually indulging or overdoing certain substances, but they tended to view the products themselves as not physically addictive. Times have changed, and our attitudes toward drugs and drug use have altered dramatically.

Take smoking, for example. While the habit has plummeted since the 1940s, when it was considered fashionable (67 percent of adult males smoked during the 1940s and 1950s), nowadays only 20 percent of adults smoke, the majority of younger practitioners doing so mostly for nonconformity rather than for its effects. By contrast, alcohol consumption remains high, particularly among adolescents and young adults (today around two thirds of Americans over twelve claim to have had at least one drink in the last year). Also, among people ages twenty-one to twenty-five, 60 percent claim to have taken an illegal drug at least once—overwhelmingly marijuana—and 20 percent to have taken one in the past month. Modern Americans, it seems, are relatively prodigious drug users, although drug addiction is far rarer—typically affecting 10 to 20 percent of users.[1]

How do we know if we are addicted? Is it, like pornography, evident to the user,[2] or is addiction more subtle, like racism or bigotry? The answer to both questions is ambiguous—in some cases "yes" and in others "no." Of course, the answer need not remain vague. There is an explanation. Simply put, evidence of addiction requires two factors: withdrawal symptoms and tolerance (that is, the need for increased doses). While tolerance and withdrawal symptoms might be less severe in people addicted to sugar, chocolate, or caffeine, or more severe in those addicted to nicotine, alcohol, or heroin, the difference is only in degree. If people cut down on or quit taking caffeine or sugar and experience mental and physical withdrawal symptoms, they are addicted. Chemical addiction (reliance on drugs), however, leads to even greater dependence, increasing mental anxiety and physical distress. Any substance that can alter the mind can be addictive.

The terms "addiction" and "dependence" are often confused or used interchangeably. Despite overlap, there is a major difference. Whereas tolerance and withdrawal symptoms may be present in both cases, dependency is generally resolved by slowly eliminating a behavioral pattern or by reducing the use of a particular substance. On the other hand, addiction occurs when behavioral patterns or extensive substance use have caused a person's brain chemistry to change. Severe addiction usually manifests in compulsive or uncontrollable urges to repeat certain behaviors or through cravings for specific substances, even in the face of doing harm to oneself or others. The only way to overcome such addiction is through treatment.

Addiction, as you might have guessed, is not limited to substances. Humans regularly become obsessed with work, performance, hygiene, responsibility, intimacy, vanity, and personal appearance, as well as to being liked, helping others, and an almost endless list of other behaviors. Viewed naturally, as patterns related to vocation, parenting, maturity, and other

1. Szalavitz, *Unbroken Brain*, 22–23.

2. Here I have in mind Potter Stewart's famous statement about pornography, "I know it when I see it."

social skills, such behaviors are not only normal but also necessary and even virtuous. In most cases, the absence of such factors can be alarming, for this deficiency can result in depression, withdrawal, boredom, indolence, and even in more dangerous and antisocial behavior such as violence and crime. However, when concerns with performance, appearance, and responsibility become compulsive, tolerance and withdrawal are clearly evident. In such cases, no matter how much achievement, approval, or intimacy one experiences, it is never enough.

Existentially speaking, to be alive is to be addicted. We all struggle with addiction, and to function without customary items leads not only to a craving for them, but also to anxiety and even physical discomfort. Of course, if addiction simply means needing something to function, such as food, water, and air, the term becomes meaningless.

## The Disease Model of Addiction: Alcoholism

Broadly understood, addiction is a universal condition that plagues not only humans but also all animal species. The use of mood-altering substances predates the rise of humans and other primates. Many animal species deliberately seek intoxicating plants or the alcohol produced in rotting fruit. Humans, it seems, discovered the stimulating properties of coffee only after observing its effect on goats that had eaten the plant's beans. Some archaeologists claim that civilization itself began when human beings settled down to grow grain—not because they needed it for food, but to make beer.

Surprisingly, the idea of addiction itself is a relatively modern concept. At first, what we now call addiction was seen as a voluntary, though inadvisable, choice. The Bible, for example, describes a "drunkard" as a "lover of wine," viewing addiction more as overindulgence than as compulsion. In the nineteenth and twentieth centuries, ideas about addiction began to change. During Prohibition, which lasted from 1920 to 1933, an ideology developed that people exposed to drugs, in this case, to alcohol, could become addicted if they drank heavily for long enough. Of course, the disastrous results of Prohibition are now notorious. Although the movement produced some positive effects, like initially reducing alcohol-related hospitalizations and deaths from cirrhosis, alcohol rates surged during Prohibition, rising as much as 300 percent. Meanwhile, the murder rate rose as well, by nearly 50 percent.

With the demise of Prohibition, the idea that alcoholism is simply a result of exposure to large amounts of alcohol began to be discredited. The repeal of Prohibition and the emergence of Alcoholics Anonymous, founded in 1935, promoted another explanation for addiction, namely, the disease model. Instead of seeing alcohol as the cause of alcoholism, experts began to view drinking as a symptom. Now the problem wasn't merely the substance but rather the user's relationship to the drug. According to this perspective, most people could safely handle liquor; only alcoholics could not. They had an "allergy" to alcohol. Legalizing alcohol, then, would allow this group to be treated medically, leaving normal drinkers alone while freeing the industry from control by organized crime. The medical model for addiction continues to be widely accepted—at least as involving alcohol and illegal drug use.

There are many controversies surrounding alcoholism, including whether alcoholism is a disease. As with the distinction between "dependence" or "addiction," or "loss of control" versus "reduced control," the answer has far-reaching implications for how people should attempt to recover. From a common sense perspective, a disease is something one either has or does not have. There is no middle ground. In the case of alcoholism, on one side of the line are alcoholics; on the other are those who abstain, social drinkers, and those who demonstrate occasional alcohol problems, such as binge drinkers.

History and science show that viewing alcoholism as a disease is speculative at best and can be used unwisely. The disease concept originated with Dr. Benjamin Rush (1745–1813), one of the most eminent physicians and authors of his day. Known as "the father of American psychiatry," Rush was the first to argue that mental illness is a disease of the mind and not the result of demonic possession. Viewing alcohol as the cause of alcoholism, rather than an individual's choice, he proclaimed abstinence the sole cure for alcoholism.

As was the case with many of his fellow physicians, Rush was also a civic leader. A member of the Constitutional Congress and a signer of the Declaration of Independence, he also served as Treasurer of the United States Mint (1797–1813). Despite his many contributions to society and advances in the field of medicine, Rush held various outmoded and mistaken views, including advocating bloodletting and purging patients to cure diseases long after their practice had declined. An early opponent of slavery and capital punishment, he argued that antisocial behavior such as dishonesty, criminal behavior, and political extremism were diseases. Believing criminality a disease, he introduced the practice of solitary confinement as a means of punishing criminals. In these views, he was clearly wrong, but his view that African-American descent was a disease bordered on delusion.

Prior to the 1890s, the term "alcoholic" did not exist. Before that, people consumed alcohol freely, though drunkenness was not socially tolerated. In the 1940s and '50s, an early member of Alcoholics Anonymous named Marty Mann used a study by E. M. Jellinek titled *The Disease Concept of Alcoholism* (the initial results of the study were made public in 1943 and fully published in 1960) to promote the disease model. The motivation—to gain financial funding by destigmatizing alcoholism and accelerating the medicalization of alcoholism—was commendable and ultimately swayed public opinion toward helping alcoholics, marginalized people, and homeless individuals in general. In the twentieth century, the validity of the disease concept was debated in medical circles, while finding wide public support. Despite its social benefits, the disease concept can be counterproductive if used to absolve users of personal responsibility, a view that can actually increase alcohol and drug abuse.

Whether alcoholism should be considered a disease depends entirely on one's definition of "disease." For instance, the National Center on Addiction and Substance Abuse (NCASA) describes a disease as a long-lasting condition that can be controlled but not cured. While alcoholism fits this definition, many acute and chronic health problems can be cured, such as coughs, colds, and flus. NCASA compares alcohol addiction to diseases like cancer, diabetes, and heart disease because, like these conditions, it results from a combination of behavioral, environmental, and biological factors. Significantly, genetic risk factors alone account for more than half of the reasons a person may or may not develop alcoholism. Furthermore, like other diseases of the body, alcoholism is a progressive disorder. In the beginning stages of alcohol use, the choice whether or not to drink is certainly present. However, as dependence increases, the brain changes, and once those changes occur, the ability to use willpower to make wise choices is compromised, leaving treatment or abstinence as the only options to recovery.

A type of substance addiction, alcoholism is less a disease and more a psychological disorder because of its effect on the reward, memory, and motivation systems of the brain. The Mayo Clinic describes alcoholism as a disorder because the pattern of alcohol use takes over a person's life. This chronic, progressive condition fits both the definitions of a disease and of a mental illness. In a manner of speaking, alcohol use does create craving—not so much in the body as in the brain. Research shows that people with alcohol dependence have impaired function in the frontal lobes of the brain. When this function is impaired, it becomes difficult to control one's impulses. For example, when alcohol dependence develops, the enzyme PRDM2 (histone methyltransferase) stops being produced in nerve cells of the frontal lobe. PRDM2 controls the expression of several genes necessary for effective signaling between nerve cells. The deficiency in this enzyme leads to continued use of alcohol despite adverse consequences. Alcohol use also affects the hormone ALDH1a1, which influences the reward system of the brain, making a person more dependent on alcohol. Mutations in this hormone may predispose some individuals to alcoholism because it reduces the influence of GABA, a neurotransmitter that acts as an inhibitor in the brain.

If alcoholism is truly a disease, one has to wonder why many cultures outside of the United States do not know about alcoholism. Is alcoholism predominantly an American disease? That would be the only way to explain why there are more alcoholic addicts in the city of Los Angeles than in all of Europe. Alcoholism is certainly a problem in America, a problem caused by excessive drinking but also by the disease concept, which leads to people to believe they are powerless in their ability to control their drinking. As history and science indicate, cultural groups that promote responsible drinking and individual responsibility over consumption have lower rates of alcoholism than those that promote the disease model.

Another questionable concept regarding alcoholism is the allergy theory, an explanation devised by Dr. William Silkworth, an early supporter of Alcoholics Anonymous. According to this view, alcohol consumption stimulates the body to create substances that produce irresistible cravings for alcohol and that result in loss of control by the alcoholic. This explanation is outdated, inconsistent with the nature of allergies, and an erroneous view lacking medical evidence. An allergy is a negative physical reaction of the body's immune system to a foreign substance or chemical. Allergies produce reactions such as rashes, eye irritations, and breathing problems. Allergies cannot cause craving, but rather the opposite; they cause abstinence. Furthermore, while allergies are detectable by a skin test, no such test exists for alcoholism. An interesting example is the "oriental flushing reflex," a response to alcohol that produces symptoms such as reddening of the skin (flushing), rapid breathing, itching, and strange sensations in the ears. This allergy, an unpleasant physiological reaction to drinking even small amounts of alcohol, affects mostly Asians. In this case, alcohol use does not cause irresistible craving for alcohol, but the opposite. This condition helps explain the low rate of alcoholism found among Asians.

Some people may have allergies to substances found in alcohol, such as wheat, yeast, barley, rye, and gluten. Other drinkers may be allergic to hops, sulfites, sulfates, and histamines. An allergy to sulfites can cause hives or anaphylaxis. Allergic reaction to sulfates might increase asthmatic symptoms in asthmatics. An allergy to histamines might cause nasal swelling and congestion. Symptoms of allergies to these allergens sometimes found in alcoholic beverages could include headache, rapid heartbeat, heartburn, nausea, or vomiting. However, the theory that alcoholism is an allergy that creates craving for alcohol is inconsistent with medical knowledge about allergies in general. The allergy theory's loss of control can only be explained as a self-fulfilling prophecy for those who believe it. How else can we explain why alcoholic priests who drink communion wine do not experience an irresistible craving for alcohol and loss of control? In their case, they think they are drinking the blood of Christ, not alcohol.

## Conceptualizing Addiction

How we conceptualize or view addiction affects not only our understanding of its nature but also our approach to recovery. Viewed as compulsive behavior that traps people in patterns of repressive behavior, addiction may be said to characterize every human being. This seems particularly obvious when the topic is examined morally, from the traditional sin-salvation paradigm. Observed morally, addictive behavior is labeled sinful, for all behavior that is self-serving and compulsive is considered defective and therefore immoral. Such characterization, however, is unhelpful and, I believe, ultimately unchristian. If humans sin, does that make them sinners? If you answer "yes," what happens when you examine the question from a less theological perspective? For example, if someone acts obsessively or compulsively in a given situation, does that automatically mean they have an obsessive-compulsive disorder (OCD)? Furthermore, if a person kills someone unintentionally in an auto accident, is that person a murderer? Surely the answer to such questions is "no."

*To think simplistically* about addiction, labeling everyone a sinner or an addict, is misguided. If all people are sinners because all sin, are all people equally saints when they perform good deeds or act compassionately? Processes responsible for addiction to alcohol and narcotics are related to commitment to ideas, work, relationships, power, moods, fantasies, and an endless variety of other things. For those inclined to think ethically or moralistically about human behavior, it might be more useful to introduce a third category, to characterize the majority of human beings as neither sinners nor saints but rather as survivors.

When examining topics as emotional and subjective as addiction, it is also common *to think stereotypically*: others are addicts, we are not; others are morally defective, we are not; others are wrong, we are right; others are lazy, unproductive, violent, promiscuous, immature, unreliable, and deceptive, whereas we are industrious, productive, calm, loyal, mature, reliable, and truthful. Ultimately, dualistic thinking and "us" versus "them" attitudes are unhelpful. Twisted stereotypes have long been used to demonize and dehumanize people of other races, classes, creeds, and nationalities, to discriminate against those different from ourselves. Concepts of addiction, in fact, have not only been enmeshed with fears about ethnicity and foreignness, but they have long been used to promote laws that target classes, races, and cultures with which questionable addictive substances and behavior are often associated. Because of America's history with slavery, immigration, and racism, many laws target members of stigmatized minorities, for whom harsh, punitive punishment is advocated.

Beside simplistic or exaggerated categorization, thinking about addiction presents numerous challenges. One of the most common is the use of stigmatizing and inaccurate language. Characterizing people with disabilities, addictive behavior, or mental illness by their condition is demeaning and discriminatory. Consequently, throughout this study I will attempt *to speak compassionately*, using "person first" language such as "person with addiction" or "person with alcoholism" in place of "addict" or "alcoholic." Likewise, when speaking about autism or bipolar disorder, I prefer "person with autism" or "person with bipolar disorder." To minimize repetition and awkwardness, I also use the expression "addicted people" rather than "addicts." If I fall back on stereotypical usage, it is due to habit and should not be considered intentional.

## Addiction as a Learning Disorder

By itself, nothing is addictive. Technically speaking, addiction manifests itself only in certain contexts. When a combination of factors in a person's social and cultural development—biological, psychological, social, and cultural—align to produce harmful and even destructive behavior that is difficult to stop, addiction is a potential consequence.

Contrary to popular belief, addiction is not solely a choice or a craving, though both are involved, and it isn't simply taking drugs or getting stuck in destructive patterns. Nor is addiction a chronic, progressive brain disease like Alzheimer's. Rather, *speaking technically*, addiction is a learning disorder, a pattern of learned behavior. Surprisingly, not all who are exposed to drugs—not even a majority—become addicted. For example, only 10 to 20 percent of those who try stigmatized drugs such as heroin, crack, and methamphetamine become addicted. The rates are higher for those who smoke cigarettes, but even nicotine addicts only about one third of those who try smoking.

Though the idea that learning is central to addiction is not universally acknowledged, it is becoming widely accepted by clinicians and theoreticians alike, going back to the pioneering efforts of Alfred Lindesmith's 1947 text, *Opiate Addiction*.[3] Since then, countless authors and researchers have made critical contributions to the learning model of addiction. To stress that addiction is a learning disorder does not mean that biology is not involved, nor does this view imply that medical treatment, including medication, is not often useful and sometimes essential. However, when the role of learning is ignored, addiction is then forced into a category of medical illness or moral failure, where it does not always fit or necessarily belong.

Traditionally, developmental disorders that appeared in early childhood, even when extreme, tended to be dismissed as phases or simple misbehavior. Now, however, stimulant medication is being prescribed to more than 6 percent of schoolchildren, by contrast with the 1960s, when it was used by less than a fraction of a single percent. How can we account for such a drastic change in perspective? The answer is that now virtually all psychiatric disorders—including schizophrenia, bipolar disorder, and personality disorders—as well as addiction, have been found to be profoundly shaped by learning during development. As we are now aware, almost every disorder that affects mental function in childhood and adolescence has

---

3. This earlier work was revised and published in 1968 as *Addiction and Opiates*.

a learned component. Since brain development cannot progress properly without experience, knowing how learning molds the brain over time is crucial to our understanding of addiction.

When we understand the importance of learning and development in addiction, many of its contradictions are resolved and it becomes easier to see why addiction is neither a moral failing nor a brain disease in the traditional sense. That's because learning produces change in the brain, based on a person's experience. This makes each brain—and each addiction—unique.

According to Maia Szalavitz, perhaps America's most influential journalist covering addiction and drugs, learning or developmental disorders display four distinguishing features:[4]

1. They start early in life. Since most brain development depends on experience, environmental influences in childhood (ranging from parental and peer influence to chemical exposures) can determine whether wiring differences in the brain become disorders, disabilities, advantages, or some mix of all three.

2. They are frequently associated with high intelligence. While developmental disorders such as Down syndrome may be accompanied by reduced intelligence, this is not the case with autism, dyslexia, ADHD, addictive disorders, or related mental illnesses. Many of these conditions are actually accompanied by high IQ.

3. They are greatly impacted by timing. Because healthy development unfolds in precise patterns, the sequencing of environmental influences, particularly social ones, is critically important. Missing an experience at one stage of development may be trivial, but it can derail learning at another stage. Indeed, at certain stages of development, notably during infancy and adolescence, the brain expects particular experiences, and if these are not delivered at the right time and in the right order, development can be skewed. If important input at one of these stages is missed, it is difficult for someone to catch up later.

4. Their progression can be changed by well-timed intervention. For example, infancy is vital to language development. Before infant screening for deafness became widespread, early hearing loss was commonly misdiagnosed as intellectual disability. Because deaf children did not learn language when their brains were most receptive

4. Szalavitz, *Unbroken Brain*, 43–45.

to it, they appeared to have difficulty with grammar and other skills. Similarly, early intervention can significantly reduce many problems related to developmental disorders such as autism and ADHD (attention deficit hyperactivity disorder). The same may be true for early intervention for addictive behaviors.

As developmental disorders, that is, as problems involving timing and learning, addictive patterns can be outgrown in a surprisingly large number of cases. Like other developmental disorders, such as ADHD or autism, addictive disorders can have beneficial aspects, such as creativity. For example, people with ADHD often thrive as entrepreneurs, while people with autism can excel at detailed tasks; many are talented musicians, artists, and programmers. Likewise, addictive behavior, frequently linked with obsessiveness, can fuel all types of success if channeled properly.

In other ways, however, addictive behavior is unlike other developmental disorders, particularly because it involves repeated choices, some of which, like taking illegal drugs, are considered immoral. Other factors, including early-life trauma such as sexual abuse, parental violence, neglect, bullying, and other forms of rejection, often play an important role in addiction. As commonly assumed, addiction doesn't happen to people simply because they are exposed to a drug and begin taking it regularly. Nor is it the inevitable outcome of a certain personality type or genetic background, though these factors play a role. Rather, it is a learned relationship between the timing and pattern of the exposure to substances or other potentially addictive experiences and a person's predispositions, cultural and physical environment, and social and emotional needs. Because it is a learning behavior, it has a history rooted in a person's individual, social, and cultural development. Addiction, then, is a coping style that becomes maladaptive when the behavior persists despite ongoing negative consequences.

Substance abuse is just one of many ways that people learn to cope. And since coping behavior is essential to psychological survival, coping methods learned during childhood and adolescence become deeply engrained in the brain. Hence, brain maturation is an important factor. As a developmental disorder, addiction is more likely to appear in some stages of life than in others. In addiction, adolescence is the highest risk period because this is when the brain changes to prepare for adult sexuality and responsibilities and when people begin to develop ways of coping that will serve them for the rest of their lives.

For example, the odds of alcoholism for those who start drinking at age fourteen or younger are nearly 50 percent—but they drop to 9 percent for those who start at age twenty-one or later. Likewise, the risk of rapidly developing addiction to marijuana, cocaine, opioids, and pills like Valium is two to four times greater for those who start using at age eleven through seventeen, compared to those who start at eighteen or later. This means that if a person manages to make it through adolescence and young adulthood without developing an addictive coping style, the odds of developing one later are dramatically reduced.[5]

Because addiction is far less common in people who use drugs for the first time after age twenty-five, it often remits with or without treatment among people in their mid-twenties, around the time the brain matures and becomes more fully adult. In fact, 90 percent of all substance addictions start in adolescence, and most illegal drug addictions end by age thirty. Given that addiction is a learning disorder, it isn't necessarily a lifelong problem that demands chronic treatment. While experts agree that serious addiction only affects a minority of those who try even the most highly addictive drugs, even among this group recovery without treatment is the rule rather than the exception.

With addiction, as in many other developmental disorders, repetitive, destructive behaviors are not usually the primary problem. Instead, they are typically a coping mechanism, a way to manage an environment that frequently feels threatening and overwhelming. Additionally, addictive behavior is often a search for safety rather than an attempt to rebel or a selfish turn inward. Because it is a developmental disorder, using punishment, fear, and threat to alter behavior that has become habitual is not only cruel and ineffective but also counterproductive. As the behavioral psychologist B. F. Skinner once observed, "A person who has been punished is not less inclined to behave in a given way; at best, he learns how to avoid punishment."[6] As psychological research demonstrates, effective behavior change is far more likely to occur when social support and empathy are used, as opposed to punishment and negative incentives. This has obvious implications for the prospects of altering addiction via the criminal justice system.

The role of learning and development in addiction means that unlike most physical diseases, cultural, social, and psychological factors are

5. Ibid., 38–39.
6. Skinner, *Beyond Freedom and Dignity*, 83.

inextricably woven into its biological nature. To label addiction as merely biological, psychological, social, or cultural is to misunderstand it.

As we will discover, love and addiction are alterations of the same brain circuits, which is why caring and connection are essential to recovery. Only by learning what addiction is and is not can we begin to find better ways of avoiding and overcoming it. And only by understanding addicted people as individuals and treating them with compassion can we learn more effective ways to reduce the harm associated with addictive patterns and substances.

## Pathways to Addiction

A common and generally misleading approach to addiction is the search for a single incident—a Rosebud moment—that explains everything. Like the word "Rosebud" in the movie *Citizen Kane*, there may be cases where this is true, and as research suggests, discerning such a moment or creating a coherent narrative out of one's experience may help recovery from trauma, which is extremely common in chemical addiction. However, as with many developmental disorders, there are often various influences and rarely a single cause. Likewise, there are many turning points in which one's developmental trajectory can change entirely. Most stories of addiction involve at least some if not all of the following features:

- temperamental susceptibility to addiction
- genetic factors suspected to increase risk of psychiatric disorders
- neglect by family
- rejection by peers
- social inadequacy, loneliness, and low self-esteem
- anger and rebellion
- peer pressure and the effects of one's cultural setting (whether permissive, dismissive, individualistic, narcissistic, et cetera)
- seeking glamour, participating in the "good life"
- needing to feel good, to increase pleasure and self-worth
- experiencing trauma, either one's own or in one's ancestral history
- needing to fit in, to feel "cool," sophisticated, mature, and strong

- partaking for "effect"; seeking to recreate the "first experience," the first "high," the first love, the first sense of power or control, et cetera.

## Five Steps to Personal Transformation

Whether one views addiction as a disease or as a learning disorder, change (cure) requires five ingredients:

1. Acknowledgment—admitting one has a problem
2. Resolution—willingness to change
3. Substitution—committing to a worthy cause
4. Human help—outside help
5. Divine help—transformative help

Such change—transformation, actually—can only take place if we embark on a spiritual journey, described elsewhere as "the second journey" or "the second half of life."[7] The key to getting unstuck in addiction lies in exchanging our compulsive patterns and behavior for one magnificent obsession, fearlessly staking our claim on the "solution" rather than on the "problem" side of life's ledger. The transformation that brings us to the second half of life is more about unlearning than learning—more about detachment than attachment, about letting go than about grasping or clinging.

This talk of the first and second half of life is not new. It has been embodied for centuries in the scriptures, tales, and experiences of men and women who found themselves on the further journey. In this second half of life, people have less interest in judging or punishing others, or in harboring superiority complexes. Life is more spacious now, the boundaries of one's life having been enlarged by the addition of new experiences and relationships. Life is more participatory than assertive, and there is less need for self-assertion and self-definition. In the second half of life people live in the presence of God. In that reality, the brightness comes from within, a reflection of the divine that is more than adequate.

For many, the second half of life is characterized by seven transformational features:

7. See my books *Dark Splendor*, 96–98 and *Securing Life*, 9–14; also Rohr, *Falling Upward*, 118–25.

- Less fear
- Less hostility and combativeness
- Less need of attention
- Less assertiveness
- Less self-concern
- Less dogmatism
- Less possessiveness

The second half of life is not about precepts or commandments, for there is only one guideline: to love the Lord your God with your entire mind, heart, soul, and strength, and your neighbor as yourself.

## Questions for Discussion and Reflection

1. In your estimation, is it better to understand addiction as a sin, a disease, or as a learning disorder? Explain your answer.

2. How can we know if we are addicted?

3. In your estimation, is there a difference between addiction and "dependence"? If so, explain your answer.

4. Discussing the nature of addiction, the author deliberately avoids defining the term. Discuss the merits of this approach. In the study of addiction, is ambiguity sometimes preferable to precision, uncertainty to certainty? If you were asked to define addiction, what definition would you give? How precise would your definition be? Explain your thought process in arriving at a definition.

5. When should people with addictions seek professional help or treatment? Explain your answer.

6. How persuasive is the learning model of addiction? What are the benefits or advantages to thinking about addiction in terms of learning and development? What are the disadvantages to framing addiction in this way?

7. Can addictions be outgrown, or are aspects of addiction permanent? Explain your answer.

8. Does addictive behavior always produce negative or destructive consequences? Explain your answer.

9. Are "Rosebud" moments helpful in explaining the cause of addictive patterns or behavior? Explain your answer.

10. In your estimation, what is the primary insight gained from this chapter?

11. *For personal reflection*: What are your addictions? How did you become addicted?

12. *For personal reflection*: Do you view your addictions positively, that is, as ways to accomplish goals and dreams, or negatively, as flawed behavior? Explain your answer.

13. *For personal reflection*: Does the material in this chapter raise any issues you might need to address in the future?

CHAPTER 2

# Addiction and the Brain

Speaking biologically, we are all addicted.

—GERALD G. MAY

THE QUESTION OF WHETHER body or mind matters more—and where the boundary between the mental and physical lies—profoundly affects our thinking and understanding of addiction. When the question is examined from the perspective of recovery—or withdrawal—one soon realizes that physical symptoms are secondary. What makes drug withdrawal unbearably hard is not the vomiting and shaking that often occur, but the anxiety, insomnia, and the sense of losing the only thing that makes life bearable and worth living. Mental and emotional symptoms, not physical ones, are the ones that really matter, the learned connection between drugs and relief and between lack of drugs and distress.

Studies show that any type of existential terror and anxiety actually heightens the experience of pain, and that the more worry and fear is involved, the worse the suffering. Pain that is viewed as life threatening literally feels more intense and agonizing than pain with a known and nondangerous origin. The source of pain is not as important as whether the person experiencing the pain believes that worse is to come. In cases where pain is associated with fear, the pain level in the same physical experience is more severe than in cases where the patient is assured that there is nothing to fear. During withdrawal from addictive drugs, fear can increase the patient's anxiety to the level of panic, thereby heightening the suffering. The reason for this is simple: whether the source of pain is "physical" or "psychological," the unpleasant aspect of the experience is processed by many of the same parts of the brain, typically neuroreceptors associated with pain.

Our society does not deal well with conditions that cross boundaries between mind and body, spirit and mind, medicine and education, or psychology and neurology. Like schizophrenia, depression, and autism, addiction has neurodevelopmental roots. Because of genetic predispositions, which affect development in utero and beyond, some brains are more vulnerable to addiction than others. Predispositions to addiction also tend to carry risk of other mental illnesses and developments as well: at least half of people with serious addictions also have another condition, like anxiety disorders, depression, ADHD, schizophrenia, and bipolar disorder. All such propensities interact with early life experience, particularly trauma, to produce risk. "Addiction doesn't simply appear; it unfolds."[1]

As stated previously, addiction is a coping style. While addiction involves choices made both consciously and unconsciously in childhood and adolescence, it is also profoundly affected by cultural factors and by how individuals perceive their own experience, particularly early in life. Persistence occurs when "overlearning" or reduced brain plasticity makes the behavior resistant to change. Plasticity is the brain's ability to learn or change with experience. Lowered plasticity means this ability is compromised, and when a pattern of activity is locked in, it is "overlearned." The capacity for such overlearning is a feature of the brain's motivational systems that evolved to promote survival and reproduction.[2]

Unlike ordinary forms of learning, however, chemical addiction involves interference with the brain processes that guide decision-making and motivation. Such addiction alters the way the brain decides what it values—for example, by making drug consumption more important than college and career, or by making all other pleasures pale. This can occur either because drugs themselves change the brain's chemistry and circuitry or because these brain systems are inherently vulnerable to being altered by certain patterns of experience.

To understand the connections between chemical substances and the brain, and why the critical period for developing addiction is adolescence,

---

1. Szalavitz, *Unbroken Brain*, 38.
2. Ibid., 39.

we need to examine the brain's development, particularly its chemical makeup.

## The Neurological Nature of Addiction[3]

Many experts, including scientists and theologians, are abandoning distinctions previously made about body, mind, and spirit. For example, neurological science has demonstrated that mind is brain and brain is body, and many theologians are recovering the old Hebrew sense that humans are beings who *are* souls rather than bodies that *have* souls. While these developments have brought a welcome holism to modern thought, we must avoid compartmentalization, for mind, spirit, and body are not precisely the same thing.

One of our problems is semantics, the old Greek word *psyche* being one of the worst culprits. While psychologists use the term for "mind" and even for the Freudian-Jungian "unconscious," theologians have used it for "soul" and at times for "spirit." Even when neurologists are precise about the brain and theologians consistent in how they define terms, when it comes to the more mystical dimensions of human spirit, those transcending the body and reflecting the sacred, neuroscientists, philosophers, and theologians struggle mightily. For when philosophers and theologians speak of the human spirit, they view it as pervasively indwelling yet rooted in the eternal; like God, it has both qualities of immanence and transcendence.

When we speak of the human brain, however, we can be somewhat more precise. Like other parts of the body, the human brain is composed of cells. There are various kinds of cells in the brain, but the most significant are nerve cells or neurons. Each neuron is a living being, for it has its own unique life and experience. Yet each neuron responds to the activities of cells and substances in its environment. Neurons both initiate and respond to a wide variety of electrical and chemical stimuli. While the brain has a limited capacity for regeneration, meaning that neural pathways in the brain can be created throughout the life of an individual, even during one's old age, the vast majority of neurons in the brain are formed by the time of birth.

The brain may be viewed as a "colony" in which billions of these tiny cells live. Some groups (local groups) of neurons are located close together in the same areas of the brain and may or may not work together. Other

3. This segment is adapted from May, *Addiction and Grace*, 64–90.

groups (functional systems) are made up of cells that do work together to accomplish certain tasks; they may be located close together or at some distance from one another. For example, the cells involved in thinking may be located quite near one another in the frontal lobe. A similar group of cells near the inside center of the brain affects body temperature, while a group nearer the spinal cord governs the level of wakefulness and attentiveness. However, most functional systems involve the collaboration of cells that are widely separated within the brain. They connect with one another through a long fiber or axon.

Nerve cells send messages through connections called synapses. An average neuron has twenty thousand connections with other cells, and some as many as two hundred thousand. At each synapse, communication takes place when the axon of one cell releases a chemical called a *neurotransmitter*. This chemical passes across the tiny synapse between the cells and is received by a chemical structure called a *neuroreceptor* on the next cell. In addition to responding to neurotransmitters from other cells, neuroreceptors are also sensitive to chemicals such as hormones, which are produced elsewhere in the body and circulate through the bloodstream. Foreign chemicals such as caffeine, nicotine, narcotics, and other drugs also reach neuroreceptors through the bloodstream and can exert powerful influences on the neurons.[4]

Through an important mechanism called feedback, cells often respond to the messages they receive by affecting the cells that sent the message originally. Feedback not only changes the messages being communicated, but it also helps maintain important balances in the body. The messages carried by specific neurotransmitters may stimulate, inhibit, or facilitate a cell's activity. This vast array of interactions, in turn, give rise to human experience and behavior. All thoughts and feelings, all sensations and memories, are mediated by the transmission of electrochemical energies along the bodies and fibers of nerve cells and across synapses. Each mental function is determined by which nerve cells and synapses are active, in what sequence, and by what neurotransmitter chemicals are released and received.

In order to appreciate how the brain functions, we need to emphasize the importance of balance and equilibrium in brain activity. All brain functioning, like the rest of bodily activity, depends upon delicate shifts of balance among chemicals, cells, and systems of cells. The interconnectivity

4. Ibid., 68–69.

of nerve cells is so extensive that anything happening anywhere within the nervous system produces effects elsewhere. A change in one cell shifts the balance of its local group and of all its functional systems. These changes, in turn, affect the larger systems of the brain, and these then cause changes in the other systems of the body. Knowing something of the complexity of the brain, of how brain cells work, and the necessity of maintaining natural balances, is essential to understanding how the brain becomes addicted.

Using a hypothetical example, let us consider the functional system that helps govern your level of alertness and wakefulness. To do so, we will focus on a single synapse between two individual cells.[5] The body of cell A is located in the frontal lobe, and its axon is connected with cell B located about six inches away, deep in the medulla, just above the spinal cord. In this example, cell A's primary function is to stimulate cell B whenever we need more alertness. To do this, cell A releases neurotransmitter chemicals it has manufactured across the synapse to join with cell B's neuroreceptors, stimulating cell B to send its own messages to other cells. When it is time to sleep, cell A quiets down and transmits less, and cell B, receiving less, also settles down.

Suppose one day you become upset over something, perhaps an unexpected bill or a threatened relationship. Your overall level of agitation rises higher than normal. Cell A sends more signals, and keeps on sending them after bedtime. You have trouble getting to sleep. While dutifully relaying wake-up signals, cell B also sends inhibitory feedback to cell A, trying to get it to slow down. Sooner or later the feedback will combine with fatigue, and cell A will get the message. If you have relaxed as much as possible and allowed this process to take place naturally, sleep will come. A normal equilibrium will have been reestablished.

What happens if you decide to handle your insomnia by taking a sleeping pill? The sedative interferes with cell A's ability to send its neurotransmitter chemical to cell B. Cell B, noticing a less than normal amount of chemical, sends stimulatory feedback, trying to get cell A to become more active. Cell A may answer weakly by releasing a bit more neurotransmitter, but the sedative prevents it from fully responding. The sedative has overwhelmed the normal process, feedback has not helped, and sleep comes.

If you take sleeping pills only one or two nights, your cells can usually reestablish their normal balance without much difficulty. However, if you continue to take the pills, you will surely become addicted. When the

5. This illustration is taken from May, ibid., 79–83.

sedatives first appeared, they forced cell A to calm down. If their presence continues, however, cell A begins to adjust. By changing its physical structure, it becomes less sensitive and responsive to the sedative's effects. Soon you notice that the original amount of sedative no longer works. You have to take more in order to get to sleep. Such habituation causes tolerance. If you continue to take the increasing amounts that are necessary to get to sleep, you keep overwhelming cell A's ability to adjust. The effects of the sedative have now forced the entire alertness system to adapt. A new normality has occurred, and it feels good—until you stop taking the pills. What happens then?

Let's assume you decide to quit taking the pills. Your stress is over and you think you can get back to normal on your own. Once the sedatives disappear from your brain, cell A, now accustomed to large amounts of the sedative, literally goes crazy when it experiences none at all. It responds by firing up to an extreme degree, manufacturing and releasing great quantities of the wake-up neurotransmitter. These molecules come raging across the synapse, invading cell B's receptors, which are now much greater in number and much more sensitive. The effect on cell B is cataclysmic. Its messages to other cells are unintelligible and out of control.

How does your body respond? You become agitated. Stress signals are sent into body control centers deep in your brain; your heart beats faster, your temperature rises, your muscles tighten and twitch, and your thoughts race. Countless other systems of cells that have become accustomed to the presence of the sedative start reacting to the stress. Cell systems in your frontal and temporal lobes, systems accustomed to the presence of the sedative, now start yelling for a fix. "Take more!" they shout, while other frontotemporal systems counter with, "You shouldn't, you'll become addicted!" The addiction, unfortunately, has already occurred.

Chemicals like sedatives can be addictive because they affect the brain directly. Some substances have chemical components identical to the body's own natural neurotransmitter chemicals, and this makes such substances extremely addictive. For example, the body creates natural pain-relieving neurotransmitter chemicals called endorphins and enkephalins. When a substance like morphine, which has the same kind of chemical structure, is taken into the body, it immediately joins with these receptors, and its effects are extreme. Similar natural receptors exist for certain stimulants and tranquilizers. Chemicals like morphine and amphetamines, which create sensations of pleasure and relief from pain while also directly affecting natural neuroreceptors, are the most addictive of all known substances.[6]

While chemical substances explain addiction, the same kind of cellular dynamics apply to nonsubstance addictions. If we had been talking about addiction to money, power, or relationships, we would have said much the same about what happens to our nerve cells. We would probably be speaking of different systems of cells, but the patterns of feedback, habituation, and adaptation would be essentially the same.

In prolonged addictions, what may initially have involved a rather simple change in a few million synapses has progressively expanded to affect billions of cells in countless other functional systems. One after another, each system has tried to defend against the initial imbalance, failed, and adapted by establishing a new normality. In turn, this causes an imbalance in the next system, and on the process goes. It is not so difficult to understand how addictions come to rule our lives. Each major addiction involves not only the primary attachment itself but also the involvement of multiple other systems. Addiction is never simple; as soon as we try to break a real addiction, it becomes a way of life. The longer an addiction continues, the more entrenched it becomes. Some behaviors or chemicals may produce a rapid and powerful effect that can result in addiction after only one or two experiences. Others may require multiple experiences before they become entrenched. But regardless of how an addiction begins, the longer it lasts, the more powerful it becomes.

As we have seen, the process of attachments takes place psychologically as a form of learning. This learning happens through reinforcement and conditioning, and it is accompanied by physical and chemical changes in the brain and elsewhere in the body. Since multiple functional systems are involved, the learning becomes entrenched.

Sadly, the brain never completely forgets what it has learned. Years after a major addiction has been conquered, the smallest association, the tiniest taste, can fire up old cellular patterns once again. From the standpoint of psychology, this means we can never become so well adjusted that we can stop being vigilant. From a neurological viewpoint, it means the cells of our recovery systems can never eradicate the countless other systems that have been addicted. From a spiritual perspective, it means that no matter how much grace we receive, we remain forever dependent upon its continuing flow.

6. Ibid, 82–83.

## The Adolescent Brain[7]

The teenage brain is not simply an immature adult brain. It is undergoing a transition comparable in magnitude to the explosive development in the first few years of life. This stage is critical for understanding addiction, for 90 percent of all addictions begin during adolescence.[8] While the size of the brain grows almost 95 percent of its adult size early in life, between birth and the age of five, from puberty until around age twenty-five the brain undergoes a remodeling that is almost as extensive as the period of rapid change in the first five years. Because the brain is in flux, what is learned during adolescence shapes both the brain and the psychological coping skills people rely on for the rest of their lives.

Importantly, both adolescence and infancy are marked not only by growth but also by a process of pruning, characterized by a selective reduction in both the number of connections between cells and in the number of cells themselves. Such pruning also occurs during early childhood, when the brain grows billions of pathways and then prunes nearly half of them. During adolescence, grey matter (the cell bodies of neurons themselves) actually shrinks significantly, most notably in the prefrontal cortex, which does not complete its development until around age twenty-five. During development, the pruning of brain overgrowth is just as important as the addition of new cells and faster connectivity. While we tend to think that more brain cells is always better, failure to remove excess cells can actually lead to disabilities. One of the most consistent findings in autism, for example, is early brain overgrowth, with some regions being "hyperconnected" or simply having too many cells and too many links between them. Though this excess might have some potentially positive effects—like improved memory or enhanced perception—it can also lead to sensory overload or to "overlearning," where a person becomes locked into behavior that becomes repetitive and difficult to change. Both overload and overlearning can predispose people to compulsive behaviors, including addictions; overload creates a desire to escape, and overlearning rapidly creates habits.

Successful adolescent development requires a drive for novelty and social contact with same-age peers. These drives are designed to pull teens away from family and toward friends and potential partners. During the teenage years, the motivational systems must also learn to handle the

---

7. This segment is adapted from Szalavitz, *Unbroken Brain*, 97–120.
8. Ibid., 97.

hormones that make these years famously difficult. Unfortunately, the last brain areas to develop are those that modulate our feelings and desires, the circuits that allow us to think critically, plan wisely, and master our urges and ourselves.[9]

The systems that underlie motivation—dependent primarily on the neurotransmitter dopamine in a particular circuit in the midbrain—play a devastating role on prepubescent youth. A change in dopamine levels draws formative youth away from familiarity and routine and makes new, exciting, and dangerous experiences incredibly attractive. As dopamine circuits become rewired, previously reliable pleasures of childhood lose their appeal.

While reward regions of the brain are maturing, pleasure becomes both increasingly attractive and harder to achieve. This occurs because during adolescence, new experiences spur larger bursts of dopamine than in childhood. The changes occurring during adolescence not only increase the need for pleasure but also produce symptoms of boredom and depression. Changes in dopamine signaling during adolescence contribute to frequent mood swings, enticing teens toward thrill seeking and risk-taking activities. These changes heighten interest in social life and sexuality by altering the way the brain responds to signals about risk, reward, and punishment.

Social approval—the biggest prize at this age—can neutralize other incentives at this time, the prize far outweighing thoughts of the future and potential risks. If adolescents think that speeding, smoking, or cutting class can win social approval, this can mitigate considerations of crashes, cancer, or college. Furthermore, if the opportunities ahead offer reduced pleasure, teenagers might not see them as rewarding at all. In fact, the adolescent brain responds to small rewards as though they were insults or punishments, which may explain some of the ingratitude and sarcasm teens display when adults praise them or meet their needs. A motivational system that is prone to boredom and places such high value on big rewards is bound to result in undesirable behavior. Consequently, many adolescents use illegal drugs not only to get pleasure but, more importantly, as a path to popularity.

Significantly, drugs also affect dopamine levels. Any pleasurable drug or experience directly or indirectly influences the dopamine-driven circuitry of motivation. And since the brain's motivational systems are being optimized during adolescence, it is not surprising that exposure

9. Ibid., 99.

to potentially addictive drugs and experiences might heighten their risk factor. Chemically, drugs alter dopamine levels, making it more likely to become dependent on this artificial stimulant. Psychologically, if drugs are used to cope at a time when one is learning healthy ways to manage social challenges, one doesn't develop better alternatives but rather heightens the likelihood of getting addicted.

Fortunately, openness to risk is also openness to learning. The same plasticity that makes the adolescent brain vulnerable to bad influences also makes it flexible and able to learn rapidly in ways that may never occur again. While curiosity and boldness can be dangerous, they can also lead to great achievement, original ideas, and new discoveries. However, a brain primed for learning is also a brain primed for addiction.

When teenagers use drugs or participate endlessly in repetitive behavior such as video games or in dependence on social media, they do so not only to alleviate boredom and heighten sensation, but also to demonstrate rebellion and proclaim independence. Often, such behavior is undertaken as much for its symbolic value in separating from parents as in its ability to heighten pleasure. For this reason, cultures that introduce youth to moderate forms of drinking or gaming at early ages or to drugs in sacred ceremonial contexts as rites of passage may display wisdom now largely lost.

Dopamine, found in only a small percentage of the brains' cells, is a much misunderstood neurotransmitter. Seeing dopamine as the brain's way of producing pleasure oversimplifies and misrepresents its role. While it acts as a stimulant, fueling craving and making drugs addictive, dopamine also reduces anxiety. Dopamine, however, has a second function—motion as well as emotion. Because many of the brain's dopamine neurons are involved in the control of movement, loss of dopamine is responsible for Parkinson's disease, which destroys dopamine cells primarily involved in motor control. Although Parkinson's is often associated with peculiar behavior such as shaking, rigidity, and difficulty with walking, it is also accompanied by psychological and emotional effects such as depression, lack of motivation, and loss of pleasure. As the illness progresses, the entire dopamine system may be affected.

Furthermore, the link between problems with movement and problems with motivation is central to how humans express their drives and desires, in other words, to their free will. For this reason, dopamine dysfunction creates not only excess movement, but also excess and aberrant motivation. This means that dopamine is involved not only in movement but also in the will or even the desire to move. To see why, we need to fine-tune our understanding of the concept of pleasure.

Research now shows that there are at least two distinct varieties of pleasure, both chemically and psychologically distinct in terms of their effects on motivation. These types, originally labeled "pleasures of the hunt" and "pleasures of the feast" by psychiatrist Donald Klein, are vastly different and must be kept distinct if we are to understand what goes wrong in addiction and the role dopamine plays in addictive learning.

- *"Wanting,"* associated with "pleasures of the hunt": excitement, desire, stimulation, intent, and confidence in being able to achieve what one wants. Applied to drug use, *stimulants* like cocaine and methamphetamine involve "wanting" and imitate the hunt.

- *"Liking,"* associated with "pleasures of the feast": satisfaction, comfort, relaxation, attainment, and sedation. Applied to drug use, *depressants* like opioids and heroin involve "liking" and imitate the feast.[10]

While original research associated dopamine with all types of pleasure, finding drugs to be addictive because they elevated dopamine far beyond its natural range, current research reveals that only one type of pleasure gets elevated with dopamine—and this creates an unusual problem. The distinction between "wanting" and "liking" is especially important in addiction because each type has a different influence on learning. "Wanting" is critical to learning while "liking" is less so. Desire fuels learning, whether it is normal learning or the pathological "overlearning" that occurs in addiction.

While dopamine is involved in motivation or the pleasures of the hunt, this is only one way we can feel good. Dopamine is not necessary, it seems, for enjoying sweetness, comfort, satiation, and serenity—these pleasures are more strongly linked to the brain's natural opioids, or heroin-like chemicals, instead of to dopamine. And this has implications for the broader understanding of addiction.

To understand why, we have to examine two antithetical effects of pleasure, tolerance and sensitization. When dopamine levels are artificially elevated, as when taking drugs like cocaine, they cause such intense pleasure that they compel people to repeat the experience, far more than natural rewards like sex or sugar can do. This creates craving for more. The brain, however, is designed to stay in a specific range of chemical balance, which

10. Ibid., 112–13.

is critical for survival. This means that with drugs, the amount needed to attain euphoria will increase as the brain tries to restore normalcy.

Over time, these opposing processes cause *tolerance*, meaning that more of the drug is needed to get to the ecstatic peaks. Increased changes in the threshold for dopamine action will cause ordinary pleasures to increasingly pale by comparison. Once an addicted person has elevated tolerance, simply experiencing a normal range of feeling requires taking the drug more frequently and in higher doses, countering the low levels of dopamine demanded by the body's opposing processes. In this case, normalcy has been redefined. To feel okay, that is, "to get high," requires "borrowing" pleasure from one's future, from an account with a finite supply. For example, just as using extra dopamine today by taking drugs requires payback in low mood tomorrow, so the bliss of drinking is followed by a hangover.

That, however, is not the total story of addiction. To complete the picture, an additional element needs to be factored, the emergence of a sensation of revulsion, of a feeling that the experience is no longer pleasurable. This is how Maia Szalavitz narrates her dilemma with cocaine use:

> I'd tell myself that I didn't want to shoot coke because I knew it would make me anxious and paranoid. I knew from the center of my cognitive brain that this was true: in the summer of 1988, I repeated the experiment hundreds of times and at least 99 percent of that time, every shot of cocaine produced fear, distress, and a severe feeling of discomfort, sometimes even an overwhelming fear of death. And yet I continued to inject coke, dozens of times a day. I did so each time with an overwhelming emotional sureness that I wanted nothing more than a shot, accompanied by an equally firm intellectual knowledge that if I had one, it would suck. I had come to truly, madly, deeply want a drug that I equally truly, madly, deeply did not like and, in fact, detested. But I couldn't learn to stop myself before I took it.[11]

The scientific explanation behind this explanation is known as the "incentive salience." According to this perspective, dopamine produces desire, not satisfaction, "wanting" but not "liking." It suggests that elevating dopamine with drugs like cocaine leads to escalating desire, not escalating pleasure. The wanting type of pleasure, however, is not the whole story. One can actually end up wanting more and more of something (or someone) that one likes less and less. Such an effect, antithetical to tolerance, is

11. Ibid., 115.

known as *sensitization*. If dopamine represents pleasure, then sensitization should make the drug feel better and better at lower doses. Sensitization, however, doesn't work this way; it makes addicted people feel worse, not better, at lower doses. Craving increases, but not pleasure. Sensitization escalates desire but not satisfaction—"wanting" but not "liking." Tolerance, in contrast, nullifies the "high" if the dosage is not varied and escalating. Both processes can feed a cycle that only makes the problem worse.

Sensitization and tolerance are fundamental properties of the nervous system, and are critical parts of normal leaning and motivation. Sensitization occurs when an extreme or painful signal is amplified. Tolerance or habituation, however, involves the opposite type of learning. Rather than exaggeration, tolerance is the process whereby novelty gets old and the unfamiliar becomes ordinary. Without sensitive to novelty or tolerance to the familiar, creating memories is difficult. While both sensitization and tolerance seem unattractive—they amplify fear and pain while limiting pleasure and joy—they clearly aid survival. Without tolerance, the world would be overwhelming. Without sensitization, potentially life-threatening situation would go unheeded. A balance between both processes is what human being need to cope with the familiar and the unfamiliar, the challenge and the routine. Unfortunately, that balance is changed during addiction.

## Questions for Discussion and Reflection

1. In addiction, are mental and emotional symptoms more fundamental than physical ones? Explain your answer.

2. Are some brains more vulnerable to addiction than others? Explain your answer.

3. Do correlations exist between serious addictions and personality disorders? If so, on what grounds?

4. What role does plasticity play in addictive behavior? How does chemical addiction influence human decision-making and motivation?

5. While overlap exists between the categories we call "body," "mind," and "spirit," how are they identical, and how are they distinct?

6. In your own words, explain how addictive patterns occur in the brain. In your answer, make sure to explain the role of neurotransmitters, neuroreceptors, feedback, and equilibrium in brain activity.

7. Why do most addictive patterns start in adolescence?

8. Discuss the role of dopamine in the adult brain.

9. Discuss the difference between "wanting" and "liking" and their effect on learning, motivation, and drug use.

10. In your estimation, what is the primary insight gained from this chapter?

11. *For personal reflection*: Does this chapter raise any issues you might need to address in the future?

# CHAPTER 3

# Types of Addiction

As we think about the forces that lead many into destructive addictive behavior,we have to consider not only the personal limitations of such individuals but also the limitations of society in general.

—JEFFERSON A. SINGER

WHEN I PONDER THE forms addiction takes, I remember the opening words of Elizabeth Barrett Browning's memorable sonnet, "How do I love thee? Let me count the ways," for, of course, the ways of addiction, like love, are countless. The list of narcotic drugs alone is staggering. The variety of addictions other than alcohol, cigarettes, marijuana, and narcotic drugs is reflected in numerous online lists. One site, titled "8 Common Behavioral Addictions," identifies categories we discuss below—gambling, sex, the Internet, video games, and binge eating—but also adds shopping, plastic surgery, and risky behavior to the list. Another site includes surprising choices among its "Top 10 Human Addictions," ranking them in reverse order of priority: (10) laziness; (9) sitting down; (8) getting one's way; (7) trivia; (6) amusement/escapism; (5) idolization; (4) sex; (3) being cool; (2) technology; and (1) being right.

Reduced to the level of a common denominator, one could argue that addiction is a universal human behavior. Nevertheless, when given options, particularly regarding substance addiction, humans tend not to slip into addictive behavior. This is why, no matter how many times we hear that a new drug is "more addictive than heroin," or that "one pill gets you hooked for life," the vast majority of people who take it do not become addicted. While adolescents are particularly vulnerable, adults with decent jobs, strong relationships, and good mental health rarely give all that up for intoxicating substances or related addictive behaviors. Rather, addictive behavior is intensified if you are immature, unsettled, or in transition, but primarily if the rest of your life is broken.

## Addiction and Personality Disorders

While most people with addictive behaviors show no signs of being mentally or emotionally disturbed, the great majority of severely addicted individuals also suffer from some type of personality disorder (PD), including paranoid, bipolar, antisocial, borderline, avoidant, dependent, and/or obsessive-compulsive disorders. Other addicted individuals, such as some gamblers and substance abusers, seem to be mainly neurotic, indulging in low frustration tolerance (LFT). Because they like some substance or activity very much, they insist that they absolutely must indulge in it, even when they "know" how harmful their indulgence is to themselves and their loved ones.

Practically all humans are both born and reared with strong tendencies to neuroticize themselves.[1] Unfortunately, certain activating events or traumatic adversities occur in their lives, and they adopt dysfunctional or irrational beliefs about these, such as: (1) "I *absolutely must* perform well and be lovable or I will be worthless"; (2) "Other people *absolutely must* treat me kindly and fairly or they are worthless"; (3) "Conditions under which I live *absolutely must* be comfortable and not too painful or else my existence is intolerable and horrible." When people invent—and believe—such attitudes, as all of us do at times, they create neurotic consequences that take the form of self-defeating beliefs (e.g., obsessive thoughts), destructive feelings (e.g., panic and depression), and dysfunctional behaviors (e.g., severe inhibitions and compulsions).

When people are "normal neurotics," and do not have personality disordering addictions, they exhibit two main forms of low frustration tolerance:

---

1. Ellis, *Overcoming Destructive Beliefs, Feelings, and Behaviors*, 357.

- Primary LFT: "I like this harmful substance (alcohol, cocaine, cigarettes) or this activity (gambling, watching television, video gaming) very much and therefore I *absolutely must* have it, no matter what its disadvantages are. I can't stand being deprived!"

- Secondary LFT: "I utterly hate discomfort and pain that result from my neurotic feelings (e.g., panic, depression). I *absolutely must* not experience them! I have to stop blaming myself for the failures and rejections that accompany them. I must indulge in some substance or activity that is immediately gratifying, that distracts me from my pain, and that temporarily makes me feel good!"

While we are all prone to addictive patterns of thought or to compulsive behavior, people with severe PD are more susceptible to addiction than are "normal neurotics," for the following reasons. (1) They have more adversities and disturbed consequences than the rest of us neurotics. (2) They are therefore more frustrated than people without PD. (3) Because of their greater and often overwhelming frustrations, many develop unusual degrees of LFT. (4) Because of their greater failures and rejections, many also develop neurotic self-damnation about their deficits, handicaps, and failings. (5) Some, for biological reasons, may be prone to excessive demands that they must not be frustrated and that they must perform well. (6) For biological and experiential reasons, persons with PD often feel so disturbed that they are compulsively driven to alcohol, illegal drugs, food, gambling, and other addictions to temporarily allay their disordered thoughts, feelings, and actions. (7) Some may be afflicted with obsessive-compulsive disorders (OCD) or have neurological anomalies that interfere with normal appetite- and desire-controlling brain centers and that decrease their ability to stop their compulsive indulgences.[2]

To make matters worse, individuals with the dual diagnosis—the combination of PD and addiction—will tend to addict themselves more frequently, have more severe addictions, and be more resistant to giving up their addictions than people without mental illness. Their resistance to change results from various biosocial factors, such as (1) their long history of being severely disturbed; (2) their history of poor social relationships, including with helpers and therapists; (3) their innate and acquired LFT that interferes with their therapy; (4) their friendships and partnerships with other addicted individuals; (5) their neurotic damning of themselves

2. Ibid., 358–59.

for their addictions, other failings, and social rejections; and (6) their deep-seated feelings of worthlessness and hopelessness.

## The Brain: A Pattern-Finding Machine

As mind and brain research reveals, not only human brains but even animal minds evolved as prediction machines—seeking patterns in the environment that would help the organism maximize the time and minimize the energy spent obtaining important resources. As a result, the human brain experiences "pattern finding" in and of itself rewarding.[3] Many of humanity's greatest creative and scientific achievements have probably been driven by this tendency, by our desire to seek order in chaos and feel joy when we find a new way of making sense. One of the greatest pleasures of music, for example, is the interplay between predictable and pleasant patterns and moments of unexpected but harmonious surprise. These joys, like those of drugs, gambling, or video gaming, play out in the brain in part through the presence of dopamine. The neurotransmitter is released in in motivation circuits when our brains make accurate predictions of a pattern.

The love of patterns and the ability to take pleasure in detecting and predicting them can lead humans to success in areas as varied as the arts, medicine, science, programming, and engineering. It also explains why games remain popular entertainment and why mystery stories are so compelling.

Gambling addiction can also be seen as one of the clearest expressions of this phenomenon. For instance, in pure games of chance, winning occurs completely at random—and there is no doubt that some people are prone to becoming compulsively engaged with such games. Just as with heroin or cocaine addiction, gambling addicts risk their relationships, homes, jobs, and freedom simply to continue to play. Internet games—or even social media like Facebook and Twitter—are also characterized by both intermittent reinforcement and addictive qualities, as anyone who has ever been annoyed by someone else's refusal to disengage from these media or by their own inability to stop watching videos of pets or of driving accidents can attest. In extreme cases, gaming and Internet addictions have resulted in disruptions in relationships and work that are every bit as serious as drug addictions.

---

3. Szalavitz, *Unbroken Brain*, 128.

However, there is no drug in these situations to neurochemically alter self-control, no substance to "hijack" the brain's reward system or directly elevate dopamine levels outside their normal range. Simply by creating an unpredictable pattern of highs and lows, gambling and other behavior can become addictive, and the fact that this occurs without a drug offers insight into why risk of addiction exists at all. A pattern-seeking brain is prone to getting fooled by random rewards that only appear linked with behavior; attempting to find structure in intermittent reinforcement can get us stuck looking for order that doesn't exist.

This helps explain why many compulsive gamblers develop superstitions like lucky charms, numbers, persons, or situations, even though the notion that these can affect the outcome is illusory. As behavioral addictions prove, many brain changes occur without drugs. And even with drugs, brain changes don't occur automatically. What matters is the pattern of use, the user's prior history and brain wiring, and the cultural context of use. Irregular and varied dosing—another element of unpredictability—is also important in producing sensitization and tolerance to addictions. As previously noted, sensitization escalates desire but not satisfaction—"wanting" but not "liking." Tolerance, in contrast, does not have this effect; it nullifies the "high" if the dose or activity remains the same. Both processes can feed a cycle that only makes the problem worse. The timing, setting, and consistency of use or activity can actually affect sensitization and tolerance so dramatically that one dose of a particular drug can produce the exact opposite effect with another. This is one reason why maintenance treatment or regularly scheduled medical use of a drug carries far lower risk for addiction than recreational use does, which is hugely affected by irregularity of supply, dosing, and timing.

Humans, it seems, get addicted only in certain contexts. As we have seen, by itself, nothing is addictive. Addiction only develops when vulnerable people interact with potentially addictive experiences at the wrong time, in the wrong places, and in the wrong pattern for them. It is a learning disorder because this combination of factors intersects to produce harmful and destructive behavior that is difficult to stop.

## Six Addictive Disorders

Our purpose in this segment is not to enumerate a comprehensive list of potentially addictive patterns or behaviors but rather to examine selective addictive activities as a means of answering the thorny questions, "What does it mean to be addicted?" and "Can people know if they are addicted?" Addiction, of course, comes in many shapes and sizes and has multiple "causes," several of which tend to overlap and interact with each other. While the discussion below focuses on "normally addicted" individuals, it occasionally includes people with PD.

### 1.  *Alcohol and drug abuse.*

While it can be tempting to try an addictive substance for the first time, things can easily spiral out of control, particularly in the case of drug and alcohol abuse. As we learned in chapter 2, when people consume a substance such as cocaine or alcohol, they begin to build a tolerance, meaning they need to use larger amounts of the substance to achieve the same effects as when they started. Prolonged substance abuse can result in a dangerous cycle of addiction, where individuals need to continue using drugs or drinking alcohol in order to avoid the uncomfortable symptoms of withdrawal. By the time they realize they have a problem, the drug or alcohol has already seized control, causing them to prioritize its use over everything else in their lives.

People don't plan to become addicted. There are countless reasons why they might try a substance or behavior, including curiosity, peer pressure, or to alleviate trauma, abuse, rejection, or pain. Children who grow up in environments where drug or alcohol abuse exists have a greater risk of developing a substance abuse disorder later in life. Studies estimate that genetics is also a factor, accounting for 40 to 60 percent of a person's likelihood of developing a substance use problem.[4] As we have seen, teens and adults with mental disorders are more likely to develop substance abuse patterns than the general population.

Excessive substance abuse affects many parts of the body, but the organ most impacted is the brain. When people consume a substance such as drugs or alcohol, their brain produces large amounts of dopamine, which triggers the brain's reward system. After repeated drug use, the brain is unable to produce normal amounts of dopamine on its own. This means that when they are not under the influence of drugs or alcohol, such people will struggle to find enjoyment in activities like spending time with family and friends.

4. *DSM–5*, 494.

Alcoholism is common in our society. In the United States, its prevalence is estimated to be 4.6 percent among twelve-to seventeen-year-olds and 8.5 percent among adults. Rates are higher among adult men (12.4 percent) than among adult women (4.9 percent). Among adults, alcoholism is greater among Native Americans (12.1 percent) than among whites (8.9 percent), African Americans (6.9 percent), and Asian Americans (4.5 percent).[5] Significantly, alcohol use also increases the likelihood of developing substance use disorders. Since alcohol is a depressant, mixing it with another drug can be detrimental to one's health. No one should ever drink large amounts of alcohol when taking prescription medications, especially opioids, anxiety pills, or sleeping pills. All of these drugs are sedatives and mixing them with alcohol can cause profound drowsiness, respiratory depression, and even death.

Among the most common drug and alcohol combinations are cocaine and alcohol use, common among drug users because of the powerful highs that both substances produce. Cocaine is a stimulant that increases blood pressure, heart rate, and alertness. This helps alcohol reach the brain quicker. Mixing cocaine and alcohol produces intense feelings of pleasure, but it also heightens the risk factors, which include heart attack, overdose, and death. Mixing heroin with alcohol is also incredibly risky. Because both heroin and alcohol are depressants, they can cause similar side effects, such as slowing breathing to a life-threatening extent. Because heroin is a highly addictive drug, it can prove difficult to quit. The consumption of both heroin and alcohol can also lead to overdosing, a recipe for disaster.

Like cocaine, ecstasy is a stimulant that can cause severe adverse reactions when consumed with other substances, particularly alcohol. The powerful high experienced while taking ecstasy influences people to drink large amounts of alcohol in a short period. This can trigger extreme dehydration, among other side effects such as diarrhea, excessive sweating, heat stroke, nausea, and vomiting.

Because marijuana and alcohol are depressants, combining them increases the likelihood of an overdose. Both substances can cause dizziness, nausea, vomiting, high anxiety, and paranoia. However, since marijuana reduces symptoms of nausea, it may prevent the body from vomiting alcohol. This can cause alcohol to remain in the system and potentially lead to alcohol poisoning.

5. Ibid., 493.

Painkillers like Vicodin and OxyContin are heavily prescribed to treat moderate to severe pain, leading to the current opioid epidemic in the United States.[6] Though such painkillers are intended for limited use, doctors and pharmacists have dispensed them for prolonged use, leading to addiction. When used with alcohol, such drugs produce dangerous health conditions. Taken separately, painkillers and alcohol may cause liver damage. However, if the substances are combined, they significantly increase the risk of liver problems and possibly liver disease.

Mixing alcohol with antidepressants or sleeping pills can also worsen the side effect of each. Individuals with mental health conditions are typically prescribed an antidepressant such as Zoloft or Prozac. Mixing antidepressants with alcohol can increase depression or anxiety. This can lead to irritability, an inability to sleep, and impaired judgment. While there are risks to taking sleeping pills on their own, combining them with alcohol use can be life threatening. Drinking even a small amount of alcohol while taking sleeping pills can increase its sedative effects, producing dizziness, confusion, and faintness.

Identifying a substance abuse problem can be a complicated process. While some signs of addictive behaviors are obvious, others are more difficult to recognize. Many people who realize they have a problem will try to hide it from family and friends, making it harder to tell whether they are struggling. In these circumstances, it can be difficult for close friends and family members to prepare an "intervention" and get their loved ones the help they need.

Alcohol or substance disorder is when a person cannot control drug or alcohol use and has emotional trouble when not drinking or using. As we have learned, the solution is not one of willpower, because alcohol and drugs cause changes in the brain that make it hard to quit. Trying to tough it out on one's own can be like trying to cure cancer with cheerful thoughts. Willpower by itself is simply not enough. If you feel like you have to drink

---

6. Between 1991 and 2010, the number of prescribed stimulants increased tenfold among all ages, with prescriptions to ever younger children, some as young as two years old. In 2012, two-thirds of college seniors reported being offered prescription stimulants for nonmedical use—from friends, relatives, and drug dealers. That year, for every opioid overdose death, there were 130 opioid-dependent Americans still using drugs. In 2015, 51,000 Americans died of drug overdose—a thousand more than died from AIDS in 1995, the peak year. Two years later, the annual death toll for drug overdose was 64,000; more than a hundred a day, and the epidemic shows no signs of trending down; Macy, *Dopesick*, 135, 145, 185, 207.

or use a drug, and you are unable to control how much you drink or use a drug, then you need help.

Treatment that is right for one may not work for another. Success depends on the addicted person's situation and goals. Many people find that a combination of treatments works best, including social support groups such as Alcoholics Anonymous (A.A.), Narcotics Anonymous (N.A.), and Opiates Anonymous (O.A.), through outpatient therapy, or in an inpatient facility. The intense therapy, counseling, and supervision provided by inpatient treatment centers significantly reduce the risk of relapse. For people who have severe alcohol or substance use disorder, going to detox is a key step. It consists of medical intervention, rest, and relaxation paired with time to help the patient heal. During detox, the patient will feel many withdrawal symptoms. Some can be treated with rest while others may require medical intervention. The goal is to stop using or drinking to give your body time to get the alcohol or drug out of your system. Most people go to a hospital or treatment center if the withdrawal symptoms are severe. In such setting doctors and other experts can monitor your situation and give you medication to help with your symptoms.

With severe alcohol or substance addiction, controlling one's behavior is only part of the answer. People with chronic addictions also need to learn new skills and strategies to use in everyday life. Psychologists, social workers, and counselors can help addicted persons change the behaviors that make them want to drink or use drugs, deal with stress and other triggers, set goals, and build a strong support system. Because these addictions can also affect friends and family, couples or family therapy may be helpful as well.

## 2.   *Gambling addiction.*

A simple desire to scratch a ticket, play a slot, bet on sports, or visit a casino is not necessarily a sign of gambling addiction, but when this desire is so compulsive that you can't stop thinking about it until you take action, there may be a problem. It is estimated that gambling addiction affects between 2 and 5 percent of all American adults.[7] While many factors can lead to a compulsive gambling addiction, the results—job loss, family problems, loss of material possessions such as a house or car, health, and problems with the law—are often devastating.

7. "Gambling Addiction," online, no pages.

Do you or someone you love enjoy playing lotto, buying lottery tickets, or visiting the casino on a regular basis? Has your desire to gamble resulted in your spending money you couldn't afford to spend, breaking the law, or had negative effects on your relationships with friends or loved ones? Frequent gambling can be a sign of a gambling addiction. Gambling addiction is characterized by a compulsive desire to gamble that is marked by an inability to control behaviors when gambling. Those who suffer from gambling addiction continue to gamble (either regularly or possibly on a binge) despite negative financial, legal, and social consequences.

Many people who are addicted to gambling will do things they never would do normally, such as stealing money from family members or friends or taking part in illegal activities to acquire money to gamble or to pay debts. Despite a desire to quit, many compulsive gamblers are unable to control their actions without help. Fortunately, there is help, and treatment is available from many different methods of counseling and therapy to assist those with compulsive gambling problems.

Because gambling addiction has no obvious physical signs or symptoms that others can spot, problem gamblers often go unnoticed for many years before the signs of the addiction finally become evident. How can people know if they have a problem? If they like to gamble, there is a good chance they may have a gambling problem if (1) they feel out of control or have little control over their desire to gamble; (2) they feel compelled to keep gambling until they have spent their last dollar; (3) they hide their gambling from friends or family members; (4) they spend money they don't have available to facilitate their gambling; or (5) if they want to stop gambling but are unable to do so.[8]

Gambling addiction affects each person in a different way and treatment varies from one individual to the next. The greatest hurdle in treatment may be admission of a problem and of need for help. Compulsive gamblers often need the support of friends, family members, and other peers in order to help them stop gambling.

Treatment generally takes place either through social support groups such as Gamblers Anonymous, through outpatient therapy, or in an inpatient facility. The intense therapy, counseling, and supervision provided by inpatient treatment centers significantly reduce the risk of relapse. Psychotherapy and cognitive behavioral therapy have proven to be effective at helping those who are addicted change their behavior and take positive

8. Ibid.

action to cope with stress or other potential triggers that typically might lead to gambling. Cognitive behavioral therapy focuses on changing the poor behavior of a problem gambler into positive thoughts and behavior. The key factor is to rewire the addicted gambler's brain into new ways of thinking about their gambling disorder and their desire to gamble.

3. *Video gaming disorder and sports addictions.*

Video games are a common entertainment option in households throughout the country. Nearly 70 percent of Americans play video games regularly, spending $36 billion on video games in 2017, a number that is expected to increase in the future. Surprisingly, the average gamer in the United States is thirty-four years old, and more than half of the parents in the U.S. say they enjoy playing video games as much as their children. While playing video games is especially popular among young adults, a substantial percentage of older adults play as well. According to a 2014 Nielsen report, the average U.S. gamer age thirteen or older spends 6.3 hours a week playing video games.[9]

Unfortunately, the risk for excessive use that leads to negative consequences is increasing. Compulsive video game addiction is a modern-day psychological disorder that is becoming increasingly popular. A multibillion dollar industry, gaming attracts millions of children, teens, and adults who are looking for the thrill and action that comes with playing games either online, on a handheld device, in an arcade, or on television. Many people become addicted to the process of gaming as children, playing many hours each day while neglecting health, family, schoolwork, jobs, socializing, and other vital aspects of life.

Video game addiction can have as many negative effects as drug or alcohol addiction. According to medical experts, gaming addiction is a behavioral problem that not only modifies a person's mood but also results in the development of tolerance, the presence of withdrawal symptoms, and the development of antisocial behavior. Some studies suggest that gaming is controlling the minds of children, possibly stunting their emotional development and interfering with their desire or ability to learn scholastically.

Gaming addiction, particularly with children, is characterized by the following signs: (1) Confusing games with reality (getting stuck in a realm where the game takes precedence over life). (2) Playing video games

9. Aamouth, "Playing Video Games," lines 1–3.

is more important than socializing with family and friends. (3) Prolonged playing of video games or watching sports on television; throwing tantrums if not allowed to watch or play. (4) Spending the majority of leisure time playing video games or watching games on television; playing video games instead of playing outdoors or with toys. (5) Showing signs of anxiety when anticipating a new game or the ability to play a game.[10]

Gaming addiction, like most addictions, is a compulsive disorder, a clinical impulse to play video games repeatedly. According to experts, video gaming becomes addictive when it involves tolerance, that is, a need to play the game or to take part in gaming activity more frequently and with greater intensity, and mood change, namely, irritability or anxiety related to not getting the video game action one desires. Like substance abuse addictions, compulsive gaming has many withdrawal symptoms or stages that come when the addicted individual stops playing video games, such as insomnia, anger, and violent behavior. Because these signs are no different from those present with substance abuse addiction, compulsive video gaming can be treated with time and therapy.

Many questions surround video game addiction. How much time is too much to spend online or playing a video game? What behavior constitutes gaming addiction? These questions and their answers differ from one individual to the next. Some can play video games for hours one day followed by long periods of not playing, while others find themselves essentially glued to the gaming system most of the day. Some signs of gaming addiction, particularly in teens, include the following: (1) The teenager only feels happy when gaming. (2) The teenager would rather spend time gaming than socializing with family and friends. (3) The teenager is playing video games when asked to do other things, such as homework, or when placed on video game restriction.[11]

Like other addictions, gaming addictions have harmful effects. Not only do they prevent kids and adults from spending quality time with their loved ones or peers to gain social skills, but they can also produce adverse effects such as increased risk of ADD or ADHD due to the high interactivity of video games; learning disabilities resulting from slowed responses and lessened sensual stimulation; increased risk of light-induced seizures from video games; musculoskeletal disorders of the upper extremities from sitting for prolonged periods of time or from using only the muscles of the

10. "Video Game Addiction," online, no pages.
11. Ibid.

upper body; increased obesity due to lack of exercise; lowered metabolism; aggressive thoughts and behavior, particularly in prepubescent children who play video games excessively; poor social interaction; and poor cooperative interaction (everything is about winning).

Video games are complex, detailed, and compelling interactive activities. Some games are intelligent and imaginative, and these tend to be more educational and appropriate for younger children. However, even games that are educational should be restricted, with limits placed on the number of hours a child may play a game, the number of games played per day or week, and so forth. Steps parents can take to prevent gaming or television addiction in their children include limiting time to one hour or less per day, keeping track of game-playing time, and paying attention to any mood or behavior changes that lead to or result from video gaming. What is the state of mind of children when playing games? Are they playing because they are bored, sad, or depressed? Conversely, after playing, do certain games cause them to react poorly to others? If so, parents should consider taking away their privilege of playing that particular game. Finally, if children have temper tantrums or shows signs of anger or depression after their video game time limit is up, parents should restrict video use.

When played properly, with moderation, there is little chance that a video game will cause addiction or adverse behavior. However, when gaming limits healthy and interactive social activity, the potential need for treatment arises. Many methods of treatment exist to help those who are addicted to video gaming, both to stop the cycle of gaming and to get the addicted individuals on the right track to social and emotional recovery. Because many gaming addictions are the result of inept socialization or the result of masked emotions, most treatment methods revolve around helping affected children, teens, or adults find more productive things to do, thereby helping overcome negative emotions and reduce boredom.

Counseling is common in the treatment of video game addiction and provides a foundation for recovery success. Various methods of counseling have proven helpful, including inpatient and outpatient therapy, trust-building methods to help those who are socially inept build new relationships, and wilderness retreats to keep users away from technology. Cognitive behavioral therapy is also beneficial, for it involves retraining the thought process from thinking about video games into more productive thoughts such as playing outdoors, calling a friend, or overcoming boredom in new and exciting ways.

As with any addiction, dual diagnosis is a common problem. Many people who suffer from an addiction to drugs, alcohol, or video games also suffer from one or more mental illnesses. Dual diagnosis is difficult to treat because treatment must address both the mental health condition and the addiction simultaneously. Treating only one or the other will not lead to a full recovery. Many video game addictions are the result of anxiety, depression, social escapism, or similar mental health conditions that make it difficult for affected individuals to interact socially. Treatment centers can help alleviate this anxiety while teaching the person to interact socially with other peers.

4. *Television, Internet, and social media addiction.*

Since its debut at the World's Fair in 1939, television has become a mainstay in the majority of American homes. From the 1950s onward, television became a central feature in American life, becoming the dominant source of news and entertainment for most Americans. In each successive decade, the hours that Americans devoted to television watching increased significantly. According to a recent Nielsen report, U.S. adults are now watching over 5 hours of television per day on average, 35.5 hours per week, 153 hours per month, or 1836 hours per year.[12] For a person who lives to age seventy, that works out to almost fifteen years of television watching. Preschool children (ages 2–5) are spending slightly less time—32 hours per week—watching a combination of devices including TV, DVDs, DVR, playing videos, or using game consoles, while preteen kids (ages 6–11) are spending 28 hours a week in front of a television.

The Internet, like television, is a wonderful source of information and entertainment, and everyone knows how addictive it can be. The Internet is addictive because it sums up many other addictions, such as exposing viewers to an escapist world; to exciting and innovative technology; to chat rooms and blogs; to endless trivia; to gossip about entertainers, athletes, musicians, and other idols; even to pornography and online sex. A convenient way to magnify one's deepest addictions, the Internet has replaced the television in popularity and necessity.

In 2000, when the Pew Research Center beginning tracking Internet usage in the United States, about half of all adults were already online. Today, nine in ten American adults use the Internet. Whereas original access

12. Koblin, "How Much Do We Love TV?", online, no pages.

to the Internet was through broadband service, a growing share of Americans now use Smartphones as their primary means of online access. Today, one-in-five American adults are "Smartphone only" Internet users, meaning they own a Smartphone but do not have traditional home broadband service.

Today 26 percent of U.S. adults and 39 percent of those ages 18 to 29 say they are online "almost constantly," whereas 43 percent say they go online several times a day. Research shows that young adults between the ages of 18 and 34 watch more than two hours of Internet or mobile videos per week, in addition to the average 2.2 hours they spend tuned in to live television. Using stream video has also become extremely popular with this age group, who are now watching television primarily via streaming video services.

While television and the Internet have been with us for some time, we hear much these days about the importance of social media. While applications like Facebook and Twitter are becoming increasingly essential economic and political tools, they also allow us to stay connected with family and friends. We have instant access to news, information, photos, videos, and updates not only of family and friends but also of athletes, celebrities, politicians, and others dispensing or promoting political, social, economic, or religious perspectives and products. Pressures to succumb or conform are often irresistible.

As with most things in life, there are potential consequences to information overload, and research shows that people are just as likely, if not more, to become addicted to social media as to alcohol and substance abuse. The difficulty with instant technology is that we have become dependent upon it, integrating it completely into our lives. Most people today access social media multiple times each day, relying on it as a primary source of information. Social media has become so popular that it is rapidly replacing telephone use or face-to-face communication. Research indicates that high levels of prolonged usage are increasingly common among the younger members of society, who are becoming dependent on FaceTime when speaking with others.

Some people are drawn to addictive substances or behavior because of the way they make them feel. By nature, humans possess a strong need to be connected to others and to belong. Being accessible to anyone, anywhere, social media offers people a way to fulfill these needs like never before. People can now be connected to the world around them twenty-four hours a day, three hundred sixty-five days a year. Over time, however, this connection can become a need. The immediacy of the connection to people and of access to information can offer such overwhelming satisfaction that it can be difficult to turn away. When hand-held devices and mobile phones are factored in, the accessibility increases. Even those with low self-esteem can fulfill their urge to connect without fear of rejection. Having an online personality is easier for some people, resulting in instant gratification. In the case of children and adolescents particularly, if the amount of time spent online is not monitored by others, the possibility of addiction is heightened.

How do people know if they are addicted to various forms of social media? Are they addicted simply because they enjoy connecting with their family and friends on a regular basis? If you check your Facebook page first thing in the morning, does that make you a social media addict? Of course not! However, addiction to television, the Internet, and social media is often marked by the same symptoms as addiction to drugs, alcohol, or other behaviors. These symptoms include feeling anxiety when access to social media outlets is not available, experiencing inability to do without social media for a set period of time (such as for a twenty-four-hour-period of time), choosing television and online time over face-to-face encounters with family or friends, and letting work or other duties slip because too much time is being spent online.

Unlike addiction to drugs or alcohol, there are usually no physical side effects from lowering usage of television, the Internet, or social media. People with these addictions are battling behaviors accumulated over time, so it is not easy to cut down. However, it is certainly possible. The following steps may be helpful: monitoring time spent online or watching television; limiting time watching television or accessing online sites (one remedy may be to remove applications from one's Smartphone or hand-held device); and finding a friend or group to help with accountability. This is always important when battling addiction.

Technology has become completely integrated into our lives, and our dependence is only increasing. That is why it is important to monitor your behavior and limit your time online. Of course, there is always the option of unplugging from the technological world, as some have done, using the extra time to enjoy the world and those around them or to get involved in a social cause or project. If you have a dependency problem, commit to spend more time without your Smartphone, television, or other technology, perhaps even foregoing use on a regular basis.

## 5.  Food-related addictions.

We all have favorite food, fixed a certain way, with or without specific spices. Most of us like sweets and chocolate and drink specific tea, coffee, or fruit drink for breakfast. Does that mean we are addicted? What happens if we skip a day or change the pattern? Can we adjust, or will we go through withdrawal?

Young children, too, have their preferences, sometimes to extreme degrees. Only a certain food will do, prepared the same every time, with fits and tantrums thrown at the slightest change. Despite compulsive behavior, they are probably not addicted, nor are they exhibiting OCD, for as we all know, this is a phase they will most likely outgrow. If the pattern persists into adolescence and adulthood, however, they probably have a personality disorder, which may or may not be correctible.

Unlike addictive substances such as drugs and alcohol, food is not something we can do without. However, for some people eating goes beyond sustenance and pleasure to become compulsive and even addictive. While food addiction is not recognized as a disorder in the *Diagnostic and Statistical Manual of Mental Disorders, Fifth Edition* (DSM–5), the handbook of psychiatric disorders used by mental health professionals, the manual does recognize what it calls "feeding and eating disorders." These include bulimia, binge eating disorder, anorexia nervosa, compulsive overeating, and other conditions that are different from food addiction, though there is often overlap among these problems.

While there is no single cause for eating disorders, genes, environment, and stressful events all play a role. Some factors can increase a person's chance of having an eating disorder, such as poor body image, too much focus on weight or looks, dieting at a young age, playing sports that focus on weight (particularly gymnastics, ballet, ice skating, and wrestling), having a family member with an eating disorder, and mental health problems such as anxiety, depression, or OCD.

Serious eating disorders are best treated by specialists, most effectively by a team that includes a doctor, dietician, and therapist. Treatment includes counseling, medical care, and possibly medicine. The specifics of the treatment depend on the type of eating disorder and on its severity.

Some people are hospitalized due to extreme weight loss and other medical complications.

Although there is currently no universally accepted definition of food addiction, research increasingly supports the idea that some foods, combination of foods, or volume of food can be addictive. Experiments in animals and humans show that, for some people, the same reward and pleasure centers of the brain that are triggered by addictive drugs like cocaine and heroin are also activated by food, especially highly palatable food such as sugar, fat, and salt. Like addictive drugs, highly palatable foods trigger feel-good brain chemicals such as dopamine. Once people experience pleasure associated with increased dopamine transmission in the brain's reward pathway from eating certain foods, they quickly feel the need to eat again. Repeated overstimulation of these reward pathways can trigger brain adaptations that can lead to compulsive consumption despite negative consequences. Some researchers, however, believe it is the *behavior* of eating rather than the food itself that is addictive; they propose using the term "eating addiction" rather than food addiction. For our purposes, food-related addiction is addiction to junk food.

Processed junk foods have a powerful effect on the reward centers of your brain. The most problematic junk foods include candy, sugary soda, and high-fat fried food. As with other addictions, junk food binging is based on behavioral symptoms, of which the following are common: craving certain foods, despite feeling full and having just finished a nutritional meal; overeating, even to the point of feeling excessively full; feeling guilty after eating particular foods, yet eating them again soon after; making excuses in your head about the need to eat something you crave; trying repeatedly yet unsuccessfully to quit eating certain foods; hiding consumption of unhealthy foods from others; and inability to control consumption of unhealthy foods, despite knowing that they cause physical harm and weight gain.

While the social consequences may be less severe that with drug addiction, food-related addiction can cause physical harm and lead to serious diseases like obesity and type 2 diabetes. In addition, food addiction may negatively affect your self-esteem and self-image, making you unhappy with your body. As with other addictions, food addiction may take an emotional toll and increase the risk of premature death.

While completely avoiding junk foods may seem impossible, in some cases abstaining entirely from certain trigger foods may become necessary.

Once you have made the decision to avoid eating these foods, you may find that your cravings may also disappear. If you are unsure whether avoiding junk food is worth the sacrifice, consider making a list of pros and cons. The pros may include losing weight, living longer, having more energy, and feeling better every day. The cons may include giving up eating ice cream with one's family, giving up eating cookies on holidays, or simply doing without candy bars.

If you decide to cut out certain foods completely to overcome your food addiction, consider: (1) Making a list of trigger foods, foods you tend to binge on or crave. You will need to avoid them completely. (2) Making a list of fast food places that serve healthy foods and note their healthy options. This may prevent a relapse when you find yourself hungry and not in the mood to cook. (3) Considering what foods you are going to eat—preferably healthy foods you like and are already eating regularly. (4) Defining your goals. Why are you doing this? What are your pros and cons? Make copies of your pro-and-con list and place them in your kitchen, glove compartment, purse, or wallet. Look at them often to remind yourself of your goals and motivation.[13]

If you are dealing with food addiction, don't try to go on a diet. Put weight loss on hold for a while. Overcoming food addiction is difficult enough. Adding hunger and further restrictions to the mix will only make things harder and possibly set you up for failure. Once you have taken these preparatory steps, set a date in the near future from which point onward you will not eat the addictive trigger foods again.

Most people with addiction attempt to quit several times before they eventually succeed. If you end up relapsing and losing control over your food consumption, know that you are not alone. While you may be able to overcome addiction on your own, even if it takes more than one try, it may be beneficial to seek help. Many health professionals and support groups can provide such help. Like Alcoholics Anonymous and Narcotics Anonymous, there are free group options available, including Twelve Step programs such as Overeaters Anonymous (O.A.), GreySheeters Anonymous (G.S.A.), Food Addicts Anonymous (F.A.A.), and Food Addicts in Recovery Anonymous (F.A.).

13. "How to Overcome Food Addiction," online, no pages.

6. *Sex and love addictions.*

James is a subdued, depressed thirty-five-year-old interior designer who began compulsive sexual activity at age nine to anesthetize himself from the neglect and verbal abuse he suffered from his chemically addicted parents. Beginning with masturbation and pornography, over time, his sexual fantasizing morphed into anonymous sex in public bathrooms and with strangers he met in Internet chat rooms. His current partner is threatening to leave him and his sexual infidelities have hurt his career. He experiences intense shame and self-loathing after each anonymous sexual encounter, and he has no idea why he continues to put his personal and professional life at risk, but he is unable to stop his behavior.

Cheryl is a thirty-two-year-old public relations executive who opted out of a brief early marriage when the sexual intensity cooled. Hooked on the "high" of the chase, she pursues rich, unavailable men—similar to her rich, unavailable father—convinced she will find psychological fulfillment if she can get one of these men to commit to her. When such an object of desire does become committed, Cheryl's romantic interest collapses and she is on to the next prospect. She longs to settle down and start a family, but she cannot maintain a relationship. Like James, she has no idea why she can't stop her pattern of destructive behavior and sustain a meaningful relationship.

Both James and Cheryl suffered emotional deprivation in childhood. Both developed rituals to mask wounds that never healed. While their motivation and result—despair—are the same, their addictive patterns are different. A classic sex addict, James is more attached to specific sex acts and sexual encounters than to people. His style of relating is detached, aloof, and avoidant, thus his preference for nameless, interchangeable sex partners. Cheryl's compulsions are more indicative of a love addict. Her interactive style is relational, romantic, and enticing, yet it results in chaotic relationships. Her addiction is less to sex than to particular romantic experiences such as falling in love.

Sex addiction and love addiction are both intimacy disorders. Preoccupation with the sexual act or an idealized, fantasy relationship acts as a barrier between the addicted individuals and their partners. Individuals like James and Cheryl need specialized treatment to give up their unhealthy attachments to sex and/or fantasy in order to be present in a genuine, intimate relationship with a lasting partner.

Those who debate the existence of sex and love addiction use the claim that because there is no substance taken in, there is no clear physiological basis for addiction. This, we have learned, is incorrect. Research on brain scans of self-identified sex and love addicts show similar damage to those of cocaine addicts. To understand sex and love addiction more fully, we need to review how the brain changes over time, what self-rewarding patterns they form, and what particular neurochemicals are at play.

Neurochemically speaking, the rush we feel when we hear our favorite song or eat our favorite meal is closely related to the first time we fell in love. The chemical that creates those reactions in our brain is dopamine, the feel-good neurotransmitter. It causes a rush of good feelings when we do something exciting or rewarding. This rush can be intoxicating, leading to a desire to continue whatever caused it. Sex is one of the greatest generators of dopamine, giving a boost of euphoria. Dopamine increases the sex drive, is released during orgasm, and activates the brain's pleasure centers. During sexual activity, dopamine floods the prefrontal cortex, the area of the brain involved in impulse control and decision-making. When the dopamine system is active, pain and unhappiness are numbed.

Dopamine also plays a role in the escalation of addiction. As addicted individuals engage in more risky sexual behavior, tolerance for dopamine begins to grow. It takes increased risky behavior to continue feeling the same effects. This flood of dopamine can impair judgment, particularly in young adults under the age of twenty-five, whose prefrontal cortex is not fully developed. Chronic exposure to compulsive sexual activities can reduce natural levels of dopamine, and non-sexual ways of receiving dopamine become less effective. At the same time, addicted persons get a more intense "high" from their behavior because their brains are highly sensitized to the neurotransmitter. The more addicted individuals turn to compulsive sexual behavior, the more the pattern of getting dopamine is engraved into the neural connections in their brain.

The hormone oxytocin also works as a neurotransmitter in the brain. It is produced by physical contact, which means it abounds during sexual activity. It is also present in the early stages of relationships and falling in love. It promotes bonding in relationships and feelings associated with long-term commitment. It can increase empathy and provides an antidote to depressive feelings. When compulsive sexual behaviors occur, the rise in levels of oxytocin causes sex and love addicts to continually seek that rush of closeness felt in the early stages of a relationship. As new physical relationships start, oxytocin leads to forgetfulness of previous bonding experiences. Vasopressin, a neurochemical similar to oxytocin, is also released in romantic relationships, fostering protectiveness and pair bonding.

When the rush of dopamine and oxytocin hits, the brain begins to change. Researchers have noticed greater sensitivity in addicted individuals to triggers and cravings, which intensify response to the addictive behavior. The reason may be Fos-B, a protein that accumulates after compulsive sexual behavior. This protein accumulates each time the addictive behavior is practiced, and it can cause changes to the dopamine system.

Fortunately, the same neuroplasticity that causes the brain to adapt to the changes brought about by addictive behavior begins to change when the addicted individual stops the old patterns and begins to practice new behaviors. As we noticed with gambling, substance abuse, and other addictive behaviors, treatment is available to those who are willing to change their compulsive behavior and obsessive thoughts, either through social support groups such as Sex and Love Addicts Anonymous (S.L.A.A.) or through psychotherapy and cognitive behavioral therapy. S.L.A.A. is a Twelve Step program for anyone who suffers from an addictive compulsion to engage in or avoid sex, love, or emotional attachment.

The first step involves identifying non-addictive sources of dopamine or oxytocin. A good place to begin is to look for healthier means to receive the emotional boost that dopamine brings, like practicing self-care or engaging in enjoyable hobbies. Since oxytocin comes from physical touch, increasing amounts of physical contact through spouse, children, family, or friends may be a helpful way to replenish your supply.

To help people with addictive patterns, the goals of therapy are twofold: first, to help affected individuals feel better, and then, to help them actually get better. Feeling better is important because a common factor underlying nearly all addictive behavior is pain, the link connecting all human beings, regardless of gender, age, race, culture, religion, or nationality. Creation suffers, animals suffer, humans suffer, even God suffers. We all experience suffering, and addictive behavior is one way to manage suffering, to handle life and its vicissitudes. Of course, people endure in many ways. Some have one addiction, one secret vice or pleasure; others cope through multiple addictions, adopted cumulatively. For instance, some people with normal biological tendencies may start by simply drinking or smoking, only to become trapped in additional addictive patterns like compulsive overeating,

drug use, gambling, fantasizing, or sexual urges. When such patterns pro-
liferate, they become ways of life, indissolubly attached to one's personality
and sense of survival.

## Questions for Discussion and Reflection

1.  According to this chapter, is addictive behavior typical or atypical,
    universal or specific and personal? Explain your answer.

2.  Explain the relationship between gambling or substance abuse and
    low frustration tolerance (LFT).

3.  This chapter labels all humans as "normal neurotics." Describe how
    normal people can be "neurotic," and how dysfunctional or irratio-
    nal beliefs can influence compulsive or addictive activity.

4.  Why are people with personality disorders more susceptible to ad-
    diction than are "normal neurotics"?

5.  How does viewing the brain as a "pattern-finding machine" help
    us better understand compulsive gambling, gaming, and Internet
    addiction?

6.  How does tolerance affect alcohol and drug use?

7.  Why does alcohol use increase the likelihood of developing sub-
    stance use disorders, and why should we avoid mixing alcohol with
    prescription medications or with drugs such as cocaine, heroin, ec-
    stasy, or even marijuana?

8.  How does someone know he or she is addicted to gambling, video
    games, sports, television, the Internet, or social media? How can we
    help people with such addictions?

9.  How does someone know he or she has an eating disorder? How can
    we help people with such addictions?

10. How does someone know he or she has a sex or love addiction? How
    can we help people with such addictions?

11. In your estimation, what is the primary insight gained from this
    chapter?

12. *For personal reflection*: Does this chapter raise any issues you might
    need to address in the future?

# THE CAUSE:

## ATTACHMENT

# CHAPTER 4

# Addiction and Trauma

The more extreme the addiction, generally the more extreme the childhood history of trauma.

—JEFFERSON A. SINGER

THE LITERATURE OF ADDICTION and the opinions of current clinicians in the field of recovery suggest that the most appropriate model of addiction is the physical disease or medical model. Despite widespread experimental and philosophical critiques, this model continues to play a dominant role in how the general public views chronic addiction to substances such as narcotics and alcohol. The disease concept defines alcoholism and drug addiction as a progressive disease that results in the inability to control one's compulsive appetite for drugs and alcohol. As the addiction progresses, the individual's body becomes progressively controlled by the substance, building up both tolerance and life-threatening withdrawal symptoms. This loss of control is seen as a physiological response, the only possible solution is life-long abstinence, and the best vehicle for obtaining this abstinence is a combination of treatment involving professional therapy and the support available through Twelve Step programs. If left untreated, addicted individuals indulge self-destructively, ultimately succumbing to physical debilitation and death.

The disease model is particularly attractive to individuals in recovery programs such as A.A. or N.A. because it offer a biological explanation for

their behavior, thereby reducing their heightened sense of shame and revulsion over their relapses and broken promises on the road to abstinence
and sobriety. Psychiatry, too, is partial to this model, because it holds out
the possibility that addictions may be controlled and possibly even eradi-
cated through biochemical intervention and genetic screening.

While the disease model requires extensive medical and psychiatric
treatment, many severely addicted individuals who complete inpatient rehabilitation programs relapse within the first year out.[1] Furthermore, the
more chronic and advanced the alcoholism or drug addiction may be, the
more likely addicted individuals are to return to their prior alcohol or drug
use after discharge. Linked to the disease concept of addiction is the Twelve
Step model of recovery. While no one should underestimate the power and
effectiveness of this approach, or of the A.A. message concerning recovery,
clinical psychologist Jefferson Singer makes a convincing case for replacing
the physiological and medical disease model with the psychological and
philosophical concept of "identity" in the management and treatment of
addictive behaviors. His collection of life stories of chronic alcoholic men,
narrated compellingly in his *Message in a Bottle*, informs us that the promise of recovery lies not so much in their sobriety as in their ability to construct a personal life story designed to reconcile three existential domains
of their lives—identity, meaning, and despair.

Recognizing that many of the chronically addicted individuals he encountered at a long-term care facility named Lebanon Pines either were
not helped by Twelve Step programs or were actually made worse by certain expectations and principles of that method, Singer concluded that the
problem for individuals in chronic addiction is not primarily addiction, but
rather sobriety itself, particularly the standards, values, and expectations of
social normalcy.[2] For many chronically addicted men, the proposed cure
seems worse—often significantly worse—than the supposed disease. In
most cases, the choice to drink signals not only a desire to reenter addictive
life, but also a rejection of the world of sobriety. This realization led Singer
to change his focus in treatment, from emphasis on addiction to the notion
that people suffering from chronic addiction either had never found sufficient meaning in a sober life or had squandered any meaning they had once
possessed. As he reviewed the lives of his addicted patients, he focused on
the totality of their lives—viewing them in the full dimension of their lives,

1. Singer, *Message in a Bottle*, 9.
2. Ibid., 17.

as whole individuals struggling to achieve a sense of identity, often under the harshest and most destructive conditions—rather than on isolated aspects of addiction. As he turned from the disease model toward the identify model, that is, from physical explanations of addiction to the underlying philosophical question of meaning in their lives, recovery required that they answer the existential question: "Who are you, apart from the cover of narcotics or alcohol?"

Focus on identity and meaning highlights another limitation of the disease concept approach to addiction, for when we think about addiction as a physical difficulty, we locate the problem inside a person, making it personal and biological. However, when we think of the problem as one of meaning and about the capacity to embrace external reality, we expand our understanding to include the social realm, a significant factor in addictive behavior. For individuals do not create meaning by themselves. They acquire language, knowledge, attitudes, guidelines for emotion and rational thinking, and value judgements from society.

## Identity, Meaning, and the Life Story

The question, "Who are you?" is the fundamental question of identity. Human identity is multifaceted, forged from the attachments, accomplishments, losses, and failures of life. Identity is also an ongoing process, based on continuity of self across past, present, and future. Identity allows humans to differentiate themselves from others, while also helping them define cultural roles. In essential aspects of identity, such as definition of the self through agency (the impulse toward autonomy and separation of the individual in the interest of status, success, and mastery of the environment), communion (the striving for love, friendship, and connection to an entity larger than oneself), and personal myth (the ability to articulate an internalized and evolving life story that binds one's past, present, and future), individuals suffering from chronic addiction are severely impaired. This impairment in the areas of work, love, and distinctiveness leads chronically addicted individuals to a crisis of meaning that confronts them with the overwhelming burden of freedom, the isolative nature of their lives, and a sweeping sense of purposelessness about their future. Their addiction—a response to this crisis of meaning and despair—can best be viewed as a flight into three self-protective patterns: surrender, blind habit, and destructive behavior.

As individuals construct their life stories, these themes of agency and communion take on different degrees of prominence, reflecting the particular configuration of an individual's identity. (The concepts of agency and communion may be traced to Freud's dictum about "work and love" as the primary motivators of the healthy individual.)[3] Most individuals strive for a balance between these two overarching motives. Lives that are markedly skewed toward one or the other of these themes may be more prone to interpersonal difficulty. Similarly, lives in which neither theme is successfully realized are likely to be troubled. For people suffering from chronic addiction, the meaning of agency (and its most obvious manifestation in work and career) and communion (as it is expressed in love and friendship) are often warped in unexpected ways. How both social forces and destructive addictive patterns lead many to falter at these two fundamental tasks is a central reason why many addicted individuals fail to recover.

Aside from agency and communion, the third component of identity or meaning is the setting of one's life story. Every life story can be assessed in terms of the background values or belief systems individuals employ in their moral choices and actions. As individuals construct narratives of the specific incidents in their lives, they make evaluative assessments of society, whether the world is just or unjust, whether people tend to be good or bad, that whether love or loneliness are inevitable. These background convictions about "the way the world is" constitute an individual's perspective or view of reality. Because most people move from factual into more abstract modes of thought during adolescence, it is during this period of development that their ideological worldviews and self-understanding develop. During this period, adolescents employ reason and imagination to rethink values and patterns they have inherited from parents and other authority figures. The idealism and strong concern with injustice felt by many adolescents can be traced to their developing capacity to imagine, at least in abstract terms, a world better than the one they see around them. Ironically, for many kids the path to destructive addictions begins during adolescence. Many of them enter adolescence already bearing strong scars or difficulties from childhood. As other adolescents begin to weave a perspective of optimism and hope about the possibilities that lie ahead, these individuals begin crafting a worldview that harbors a profound fatalism or nihilism about their lives and life in general.

---

3. What Freud actually proposed was a distinction between Thanatos (a force of separation and disintegration) and Eros (a unifying and integrative force).

The meanings of life available to many addicted individuals are necessarily a function of the experiences they have undergone and the lessons they have learned from the subcultures in which they have been raised and to which they have been exposed. As we think about the forces that lead many into destructive addictive behavior—childhood abuse, social rejection, poverty, racism, homophobia, violence, war, material culture—we have to consider not only the personal limitations of such individuals but also the limitations of the world they have left and which they are being encouraging to reenter. If they cannot find meaning in acceptable behavior, is their distrust and discomfort psychological or sociological in nature? Is their addictive behavior the result of inner deviance, or is it a veiled protest against "normalcy" and "business as usual" in society, a muted denunciation of an alien value system in America primarily determined by a cultural elite composed of prosperous white Anglo-Saxon Protestant males? In other words, is their behavior essentially rebellious or prophetic?

Framing the discussion in this manner leads to further reflection. What does this say about us? As contributors to society, what are we doing to change the destructive social conditions that contribute to and perpetuate destructive addictions? Are we complicit in the extensive addictive suffering going on around us? While acknowledging our role in initiating and perpetuating chronic addiction does not free others from the responsibility they face to gain control over self-destructive behavior, it reminds us of our own role as agents of change locally and as citizens globally. No wonder many find comfort in the disease concept of addiction.

The disease model brings another level of security to non-addicted individuals. If we say someone has a disease, we are implicitly raising the question of whether we too have that ailment. If we answer "no," then we are placing addicted individuals into a stigmatized category: they are diseased and we are not. Their problem becomes a medical concern relevant to their personal health, and the rest of us remain absolved of responsibility. Focusing on existential rather than on medical issues requires an examination of addiction in a social context that emphasizes the connectedness of addicted and non-addicted individuals rather than their dissociation. Once we acknowledge that we are all in the same existential boat—wrestling with meaning in a chaotic and destructive society—we no longer place severely addicted individuals into the "other" and "not me" category. This sense of mutuality also encourages greater empathy and patience in our efforts to make sense of the world, and it reminds us that trauma, defenses, and despair are present in our lives as well.

A fundamental premise in this book is the idea that understanding addiction requires a linkage of past, present, and future. In constructing a meaningful life story organized around formation and responsibility, individuals need to see the events of their lives as interrelated parts of a unified narrative rather than as a series of isolated episodes or random occurrences. If one's story grows out of an overarching set of goals or a unifying personal myth, then what happened in the past, what is occurring in the present, and what we hope to become in the future will coalesce into a meaningful identity.

In my own personal myth, for example, I see myself as an ordained minister and a professor retired from a liberal arts college. As I look to the past, I see how my parents' careers in Latin America, whether working with orphaned children on a two-hundred-acre farm or as missionaries in theological and academic settings, influenced my career as a college chaplain and professor of religious studies. In addition, I am aware of the impact of dedicated professors who taught me literature, psychology, foreign languages, and philosophy as an undergraduate and biblical, theological, and ethical study in graduate programs. Their enthusiasm about intellectual pursuits and their commitment to liberal arts helped provide direction to my career path. My current work as a researcher and writer continues to draw upon the inspiration they provided and the models they offered in the classroom and during informal advising.

At the same time, my childhood and adolescent experience—an only child raised bilingually in Costa Rica before being sent to a boarding school in New York State, where I lived independently during adolescence with limited financial resources—coupled with an introverted intuitive personality type, helped shape my identity over time. These factors, in addition to a stable marriage, good health, a fulfilling career, and a meaningful sense of community, provided coherence and direction for the future.

Individuals suffering from chronic addiction often feel the exact opposite way. They struggle with problems of identity, with incoherence and discontinuity, their life story fragmented by a disunified past, present, and future. Their difficulty with identity is often compounded by two additional factors—the effects of trauma and of compensatory addictive patterns or behavior over time. Either element prevents individuals from developing healthy identities, but both together hinder efforts in the three main areas of identity: definition of the self through love and work, through continuity over time, and through distinctiveness and membership in beneficial community.

Combat veterans traumatized by their war experiences who then develop addictions face this exact dilemma. Alone and haunted by the past, they see no clear vision of how to escape memory and move forward. Some end up waging war on memory through addictive lifestyles. Their war is fought on two fronts—in the short term a drink or drug dulls pain and consciousness of the past or present, and in the long run a life of addiction buffers them against future engagement with relationships and societal demands.

Behind their stories lies an insight about what the construction of identity demands from all of us, addicted and non-addicted alike. To feel we are moving toward a desired goal in our daily activities, we look to our past for a coherent message about our previous experiences. To trust ourselves to take action in the future, therefore, we need to extract a sense of meaning with regard to what we have done and what has been done to us. Trauma of any kind—war, abuse, disaster—challenges our capacity to make unified stories out of the events of our lives. The nature of trauma—its disjunction with any previous reality—stuns us and leaves us grasping for meaning. When memories of the trauma persist and we cannot integrate them into an acceptable framework, when they simply won't fit what we know of the world or want to know, despair sets in. A drink or drug relieves this despair, both by blotting out thought and by blotting out the need for memory. If we can understand this, we can then understand veterans suffering from chronic addiction are not simply addicts with a traumatic past. They are individuals caught in a struggle to destroy their past and in this way release themselves from the demands of the future. Their problem is not that they have a bad story, but that their trauma and addiction drive them to become story-less, losing both identity and a sense of membership in society.

When we meet chronically addicted individuals, we must not ignore them or keep them at arm's length. They are more than alcoholics, junkies, or bums. They are human beings, like any one of us, struggling with a sense of identity and purpose.

## Identity, Trauma, and Despair

According to a 2008 study by the Rand Corporation, approximately 18.5 percent of U.S. service members returning from Afghanistan and Iraq have experiences of posttraumatic stress disorder (PTSD) or major depression. Drawing figures from Veterans Administration data, a 2011 CBS News report found some 800,000 troops suffering from PTSD. Howwever, as Bob Delaney notes in *Surviving the Shadows*, PTSD is hardly limited to the military. According to a report by the National Institute of Mental Health, some 7.7 million Americans eighteen years and older suffer from the condition.[4] This includes people from all walks of life, traumatized by stress, violence, abuse, and by suicidal deaths of loved ones.

Individuals diagnosed with PTSD, whether the result of military service or of trauma of any kind—abuse, abandonment, bullying, or other types of physical or emotional disaster—need help to find ways to build life in the present. Though they cannot be expected to let go of or forget the past, they must be encouraged to see a tangible present and a hopeful future no longer affected by traumatic memory. While research demonstrates that veterans who suffer the greatest problems with PTSD and addiction are those who entered the service already suffering from significant disruptions or trauma in their pre-combat life, preexistent risk factors should not diminish the possibility that healthy individuals, once exposed to the horrors of war, are also scarred and therefore capable of developing significant traumatic disorders.

For most of history and even in contemporary traditional societies, the question of identity could be answered by reference to a set of clear social categories. Your identity came from family, kinship groups, religious affiliation, and social class. By the nineteenth century, with the ascent of democracy in many western societies, the question of identity became more complicated, at least for men; in most cases women were still rigidly restricted in their efforts at self-definition. As the mobility created by modern economies spurred people to move from their homes, rise to a higher social class, and experiment with new social and religious ideals, the prospect of constructing rathr than inheriting one's identity became the driving vision of the century. The late nineteenth and twentieth centuries, as captured in the writings of existentialist philosophers, became a period of intense questioning about the meaning of existence and the purpose of

---

4. Delaney, *Surviving the Shadows*, 5.

life. More than ever, individuals faced a personal struggle with the question of "Who am I?" The quest to determine one's identity had become a heroic struggle to locate a sense of ethical purpose, meaningful occupation, and lasting relationships in an unstable, technologically impersonal, and spiritually troubled world.

People suffering from chronic addiction struggle with identity on at least three levels. Trapped in a body constitutionally prone to addiction, they suffer both the destructive physical and psychological consequences of an addictive existence. Secondly, their capacity to extract meaning from their troubled lives or to ward off anxiety without reliance on an addictive substance or behavior is profoundly compromised. Thirdly, both familial and social forces may have contributed to the development of their addiction and now actively aggravate their condition through social ostracism and alienation. Having addressed the first and second factors, we address this final factor in this segment.

Many who start using drugs or alcohol do so to repress painful memories or to numb the enduring pain of loss, poverty, death, violence, or sexual identity issues. In a world where career and relationships, agency and communion are the shared pillars of identity, those who feel they have failed at one or both of these may drift toward the self-destructive world of addiction. As the stories of those suffering from severe addictions make clear, the disease model of addiction fails to address issues related to two key issues in adult well-being: identity (self-esteem) and membership in responsible society.

While traits that make children stand out from their peers are often biological—estimates of the genetic heritability of addiction are around 40 to 60 percent[5]—this leaves a large opening for the influence of other factors in addiction.[6] The addicted person's environment, whether nurturing and safe or marred by trauma like loss, violence, or other factors, plays perhaps an equally large role in determining how addictive behaviors develop. People who have not had traumatic experience or studied trauma find it hard to imagine the pain of these individuals. When we consider women who fall into the most despised category of addicted people—crack-addicted mothers who smoked during their pregnancies—we regularly discover their childhoods to have been a litany of sexual abuse, physical abuse, ne-

5. Szalavitz, *Unbroken Brain*, 63.

6. The issue of temperament and personality in addiction is addressed more fully in chapters 5 and 12.

glect, death, violence, disease, poverty, bullying, and simply one loss after another. Research shows that over two thirds of addicted people have suffered at least one extremely traumatic experience during childhood, and the higher the exposure to trauma, the greater the addiction risk.[7]

Additionally, the more extreme the addiction, generally the more extreme the childhood history of trauma. In fact, one third to one half of heroin injectors have experienced sexual abuse, and in half of those sexual abuse cases, the offense was not just one incident but an ongoing series of attacks, typically conducted by a relative or family friend who should have been a source of support, not of abuse. The same proportion of heroin addicts have suffered emotional abuse and physical neglect, leading to the characterization of the typical pre-addiction experience as a "shattered childhood."[8]

This doesn't mean that all addiction comes from trauma, for substance use is one of many ways that people learn to cope. Because coping behavior is essential to psychological survival, coping methods learned during childhood and adolescence become deeply engraved in the brain. Nonetheless, the linking of addiction to trauma is indisputable. Studies of "adverse childhood experiences" (ACEs) show a linear relationship between the number of traumas and addiction risk. Even one extreme adversity—like losing a parent or witnessing domestic violence—before age fifteen doubles the odds of substance use disorders. Other ACEs include divorce; verbal, physical, and sexual abuse; neglect; active addiction or mental illness in the immediate household; and having incarcerated family members. If one learns at a young age that the world is not safe or stable, this can shape the trajectory of emotional learning and how people cope for the rest of their life. One study shows that a child with five or more ACEs has a risk of illegal drug addiction seven to ten times greater than one who has none. Additionally, the risk of heavy smoking is nearly tripled for people with five or more ACEs, and alcoholism risk is increased by a factor of seven for those with four or more. Although some ACEs may also represent genetic risk factors (for example, having an addicted or mentally ill parent can both signal genetic risk and create an unstable home environment), the relationship between the amount of traumatic experiences a person has and the risk for addiction is undeniable.[9]

7. Szalavitz, *Unbroken Brain*, 65.
8. Ibid.
9. Ibid., 66–67.

Furthermore, research shows that trauma doesn't only harm the person directly affected, but that it can be passed to the next generation. This happens not simply because trauma can affect the quality of parenting, but because it can also lead to changes in chemicals that regulate genes. Such alterations, known as "epigenetic" changes, don't merely influence parenting behavior in traumatized parents, but they may also affect sperm and egg cells, directly influencing the resulting child's brain development. Epigenetics involves changes to molecules that determine which genes are turned on and which remain silent. These changes don't alter the DNA directly, that is, how genetic information is transmitted, but they affect the structures around the DNA that determine how it is read. This, in turn, alters how active or inactive particular genes will be. What this means is that the trauma someone's parents or even grandparents experienced may potentially affect a child's brain development and, consequently, their risk for addiction. For example, studies on the offspring of Holocaust survivors suggest that their experiences may be written in their genes. While the results may vary depending on which parent was affected, one study showed that having a mother with post-Holocaust posttraumatic stress disorder increased the effects of a gene involved in amplifying stress signaling in the brain.

In the case of depression, animal studies find that offspring born to either parent that suffers stress, whether father or mother, may be affected negatively for up to two generations before reverting to pre-stress levels. In addition to how genetics affects animal offspring, stress and trauma also influence human parental interact with infants. This, in turn, potentially changes the infant's gene expression, during a phase of life when developing brains are looking for signals about what type of environment they will face. How human parents interact with infants influences their growth patterns physically and psychologically. Epigenetic signals from the parent particularly affect the offspring's stress response systems, which are critical to addiction risk, since substance use is often an attempt to manage stress.

Obsessive-compulsive disorder (OCD), often connected with addictive behavior, is also linked to fear of death, which affects some children profoundly. Worrying about death, coupled with the sense that one is powerless over such things, can become obsessive. Obsessive fear—whether about mortality or about other factors over which we have little control—is often a symptom of the obsessive behavior that is seen in psychiatric disorders such as Asperger's and OCD. Unhealthy anxieties frequently occur when a child's same-sex parent undergoes treatment from diseases such as diabetes or cancer. Over time, anxieties and obsessive fears can translate into compulsive rituals or secret defenses such as agoraphobia and claustrophobia.

In OCD and Asperger's, as in addiction, such behavior eventually stops serving its intended purpose. Rather than making things better, it makes them worse. Unfortunately, by this time, habitual responses are already deeply engrained and well learned, so even if the ritual designed to lessen anxiety actually increases it, the ritual is repeated. This is the heart of why addictions are learning disorders. Though some drugs obviously have risks other than addiction, if one looks for the cause of addiction in the chemicals themselves, the connection is missed. What matters is not the existence of activities or substances that offer escape, but rather the need for relief and the learned pattern of seeking. Consequently, trying to fight addiction by criminalizing particular drugs is like trying to suppress repetitive behaviors in autism by punishing them. Penalizing people whose condition is marked by failure results, at least in part, from a failure to understand how learning affects addiction.

It is now clear that most cases of addiction start long before affected people are ever exposed to cigarettes, alcohol, or drugs. While there are many paths to addiction, addictive behaviors develop in the interaction between childhood temperament, childhood experience, and children's interpretation of their experience. How this happens varies from one individual to the next. In Maia Szalavitz's case, for example, oversensitivity led to self-hate; this combined with a lack of other coping skills led her to find drugs, heroin in particular, overwhelmingly attractive. With her friend Ron, heroin addiction began differently. He grew up black and middle class, but stuttering made him feel insecure. He felt tremendous pressure to live up to his parents' dream that he become a doctor or lawyer—and that gave him a highly contingent sense of self-worth. Experimenting with heroin at the age of fourteen increased his sense of well-being and led to his addiction. In contrast, Violet, another friend, had an experience largely driven by trauma. Before she was thirteen, she had witnessed her father's death, lost her older brother in a motorcycle accident, been bullied repeatedly at school, and suffered at least four years of molestation by an uncle. She described her first experience of crack as feeling "like a weight was lifted off my shoulders." Her early life was filled with loss and a sense that she was worthless and powerless. She discovered that drugs not only alleviated such conditions, but they also empowered her, creating a sense of invincibility.[10]

Because only a small minority of those who try recreational drugs become addicted, mere exposure is not what differentiates between those who maintain control over their use and those who do not. Drugs alone do not "hijack the brain." Instead, what matters is what people learn—both before and after trying them. Obviously, "physical addiction" is encoded in the brain—but so, too, is psychological addiction.

If early childhood leaves us with a multitude of risk factors for addiction, puberty and adolescence, combined with experiences during elementary, junior high, and high school, turn predilections and potentiality into reality. As noted earlier, what is learned during the teen years shapes both the brain and the psychological coping skills people rely on for the rest of their lives. When we add factors such as poverty, chaos, bad parenting, and trauma to the mix, addiction risk increases. In such situations, addictive behavior that increases pleasure and minimizes pain seems to make sense. If one's experience suggests that a positive future may never come, focusing on the present is actually rational. If the world is unpredictable and people are unreliable, available reward now is more valuable than uncertain gain later. As studies show, when the future is uncertain or the provider undependable, children with the option to have one treat now or two treats later will sensibly scarf down the first sweet rather than rely on a possible treat in the future. Being present-focused and prioritizing whatever good experiences are available in the present can be an effective survival strategy in an uncertain world. However, it can also lead to dangerous addiction. And those who become addicted become less and less capable of making wise long-range decisions.

## Questions for Discussion and Reflection

1. Why is the disease model of addiction attractive to individuals in recovery programs?

2. How does the role of early-life trauma contradict or at least challenge the physical disease or medical model of addiction? Explain your answer.

10. Ibid., 80.

3. Evaluate the merits of Jefferson Singer's argument for replacing the physiological medical disease model in the management and treatment of addictive behavior with the psychological and philosophical "identity" model.

4. Why, according to Singer, are chronically addicted individuals not helped and possibly even made more resistant to rehabilitation by Twelve Step programs?

5. What does Singer mean by "agency" and "communion" and how do they influence a person's identity and, ultimately, recovery from addiction?

6. According to Singer, how is chronic addiction a critique of social normalcy, that is, a critique of "business as usual" in society?

7. Why are individuals suffering from chronic addiction often unable to construct a unified life story that adequately links past, present, and future? How does this inability to escape memory and move forward affect combat veterans and others diagnosed with PTSD?

8. In your estimation, what role does early-life trauma play in alcoholism or in substance abuse? Explain your answer. Can you provide examples from people you know?

9. Evaluate the idea that trauma can be passed to the next generation.

10. How can fear of death be connected with addictive behavior? Explain your answer.

11. In your estimation, what is the primary insight gained from this chapter?

12. *For personal reflection*: Does this chapter raise any issues you might need to address in the future?

# CHAPTER 5

# Addiction and Personality

The addictive personality is multifaceted.
It doesn't exist as a separate entity.

—GEORGE KOOB

WHILE MOST HUMAN BEINGS are subject to addictive and compulsive behavior, some seem more susceptible, even predisposed to such behavior. Are some individuals more prone to obsessive behavior than others? If so, is this due to inherited factors such as temperament and personality traits?

Nobody knows for sure what creates an individual's personality type. It seems that both heredity and our early childhood relationships with parents or other significant people are the two most important sets of influences. Heredity seems to provide us with a basic temperament, while our early relationships further crystallize our temperamental predisposition and heavily influences how healthy or unhealthy we are as we begin life. While parenting counts heavily, parenting itself is not the decisive factor in determining psychological type. Clearly, the personality types of the parents do not determine the personality type of a child. If genetics alone were responsible for determining type, all the children born of a particular set of parents would have the same personality type, and that is certainly not the case.

The innate and genetic structures that lead to the development of one's personality type are usually referred to as one's temperament. In a sense, we all have been dealt certain cards at birth, and during childhood and adolescence we find ways to build upon this foundation. Of course, the temperament we have is not the result of a conscious choice, nor is it the result of our parents. The choices we make regarding our personality come later in our development and have to do with the formation of our identity, particularly the creation of a "sense of self" that both allows and disallows certain feelings and characteristics within us. The temperament expresses itself early in life in one of three general ways. Social scientists sometimes define the temperament types as "high responders" (as eager, energetic participants in their world), "low responders" (as quiet, withdrawn, or shy participants in their world), and "in-between responders" (as compliant participants in their world).

The idea of temperament throws light on a significant issue in child-hood development, the question of "fit" between the temperament of the child and that of the parents. A high responder child can be extremely challenging to the parents if they are low responders, or if they are dysfunctional in ways that allow little energy for coping with a high-energy child. The reverse might also be true: the parents could be high responders while a child is a low responder. While parents do not determine one's psychological type or basic temperament, parents do play an extremely significant role in the child's development and overall personality pattern. While our parents may not determine our type, they certainly determine how healthy or unhealthy we are as representatives of our type. Destructive, abusive, or neglectful parents can make a major difference in the kinds of adaptations the child will have to make, as can loving and caring adults with good parenting skills.

Personality traits are the building blocks of our personalities. Traits such as anger, shyness, excitability, and empathy, for example, constitute the larger patters that make up much of our individual and interpersonal life. Cultural norms greatly influence how we view personality and character, including which traits we value or disparage. In America, for example, cultural images of addiction tend to be skewed and racialized, even though blacks and Hispanics are no more likely than whites to be addicted. Media accounts about addiction tend to portray people with dark skin, and when whites are shown, they are generally described as being atypical. Additionally, these images tend to depict people severely addicted individuals as subhuman, driven by passion and hedonism, rather than by a comprehensible search for safety and comfort. The "addictive personality" is typically viewed as morally weak, unreliable, selfish, and out of control. The temperament from which it springs is seen as defective, unable to resist temptation. Ironically, even when we joke about having an addictive personality, we usually do so to justify an indulgence or to signal guilt about pleasure. To understand the role of learning in addiction and in the temperaments that predispose people to it, we have to examine the relationship between addiction and personality more closely.[1]

Although Alcoholics Anonymous and psychiatry originally framed addiction as a form of antisocial personality or "character" disorder, research does not confirm this diagnosis. Despite decades of experimentation, no single addictive personality common to all addicted individuals has ever been found. As George Koob, director of the National Institute on Alcohol Abuse and Alcoholism once noted, "What we're finding is that the addictive personality is multifaceted. It doesn't really exist as an entity of its own."

Research finds no universal character traits common to all addicted people. Some are shy; others are bold. Some are fundamentally kind and caring; some are cruel. Some tend toward honesty; others toward deception. While some stereotypes are typically present, the entire range of human character can be found among people with addictions. Only 18 percent of addicts, for example, have a personality disorder characterized by lying, stealing, lack of conscience, and manipulative antisocial behavior. While this proportion is four times greater than the general public, what is significant is that 82 percent do not fit this particular caricature of addiction.[2]

Although potential addicts cannot be identified by a specific collection of personality traits, it is often possible to detect early on which children are at high risk. While some stand out because they are antisocial and callous, others do so because they are overly moralistic and sensitive. While those who are unusually impulsive and eager to experiment are at high risk, the odds of addiction are also elevated in those who are compulsive and fear novelty. It is extremes of personality and temperament, not deficits, that elevates risk. Surprisingly, giftedness and high intelligence are more regularly linked with illegal drug use than average talent and intelligence.

Whether extreme traits lead to addictions, other compulsive behaviors, developmental differences, mental illnesses, or some mixture depends

1. The segment on the myth of the addictive personality is adapted from Szalavitz, *Unbroken Brain*, 58–71.

2. Ibid., 59.

not just on genetics but also on the cultural environment and on other people's reactions to such traits and behavior. Addictions and other neuro-developmental disorders rely not just on actual experience but on how it is interpreted and how parents and friends respond and label such behavior.

Longitudinal studies—studies that follow participants from infancy into adulthood—indicate that the most mentally and psychologically healthy teens are not those who abstained entirely from alcohol and other drugs, but rather those who experimented with marijuana and drinking without overdoing it. Because occasional teen drinking and marijuana use is actually normal adolescent behavior, it is not problematic. Rather, the teens who became frequent users and drinkers were overly anxious, uptight, and lacking in social skills, and it was these conditions, coupled with problems such as depression, anxiety, and delinquent behavior, that made them susceptible to severe addiction. According to studies made in countries where drinking is a social norm, moderate drinkers—not non-drinkers—are the most well-adjusted. The healthiest patterns are found in the middle of the curve, not at the extremes.

In addition, longitudinal studies identify three specific temperamen-tal traits or pathways that seem to predispose youth to addiction risk, all of which appear in nascent form in young children. The first, most common in males, involves impulsivity, boldness, and desire for new experience. This combination of traits can lead to addiction because it makes it hard for people to control their behavior. The second, most common in females, in-volves being sad, inhibited, and/or anxious. While such emotions can deter experimentation, they can also provide a self-medicating path to addiction, where addictive substance can be used to cope with painful feelings. The third path involves having both types of traits, where people alternatively fear and desire novelty. Such paradoxical behavior leads affected individu-als to act inconsistently, swinging from being impulsive and rash to being compulsive, fear-driven, and stuck in rigid patterns.

Here is where some of the contradictions that confound the study of addiction become evident, for some aspects of addictive behavior seem precisely planned out, while others show lack of restraint. If we look more closely, however, the paradoxes disappear, for all three pathways involve the same fundamental problem—difficulty with self-regulation. While im-pulsiveness involves too little behavioral inhibition and failure to prevent reckless behavior, obsession and compulsion involve the other end of the spectrum—too much inhibition, difficulty getting out of a rut, rather than preventing actions from being initiated. Such traits, compounded by the inability to control fear and other emotions, also reduce the brain's capacity to self-regulate, thereby laying the groundwork for addiction. The regions of the brain that allow self-regulation need experience and practice in order to develop. If that experience is aberrant or if those brain regions are wired unusually, they may not learn to work properly.

The areas of the brain involved in self-regulation include the prefrontal cortex (PFC), which imagines possible futures and makes decisions accordingly, and the orbitofrontal cortex, which influences levels of motivation and the choices one tends to make. The PFC works in concert with the nucleus accumbens, the region known as the brain's "pleasure or reward" center. This area is involved in determining the desirability of particular options and whether to seek or avoid them. The insula, which processes emotions like lust and disgust while also monitoring internal states like hunger and thirst, is another node in this circuitry. So is the anterior cingulate, which looks for conflicts and errors and changes emotion accordingly. This area is especially important for obsessive behavior, perhaps because it creates a sense that things are "not right" until they are perfect or complete. The amygdala, best known for its role in processing fear and many other emotions, is also in this loop. Together, this entire neural network sets values, priorities, and goals.

As a behavior moves from being a conscious choice to a habit, brain activity changes, moving toward the top or "dorsal" portion of the striatum, the broader are that contains the nucleus accumbens, and away from the bottom or "ventral" area. In addiction and other compulsive behavior, brain activity that is increasingly dorsal in the striatum seems to be linked with reduced ability of the prefrontal cortex to stop or control the behavior.

One critical aspect of addiction is an alteration in the balance between brain networks that drive habitual behavior and those that determine whether or not to execute those routines. These regions are made to change with experience and, as a result, are developmentally vulnerable both in early childhood and adolescence. Any activity, such as learning to play the piano or throwing a ball, allows "muscle memory" to develop, and as people hone their skills, their behavior becomes more automatic and less conscious. The same is true with addictive behavior. The regions of the brain that make possible curiosity, focus, and ability to learn also make us vulnerable to negative and potentially harmful habits.

As we have seen, parenting and social interaction strongly shapes personality and influences self-image, as does labeling. Children take in and react to what they are told about themselves, often in unpredictable and unintended ways. These initial self-concepts shape their choices and, in turn, their brains. If children are told they are "good" or "bad," "smart" or "stupid," "kind" or "selfish," or good or bad at sports or other activities at an early age, they will form lasting views about themselves that are positive or negative. Research shows that kids of preschool age often fixate on ideas of "goodness" and "badness" as they relate to themselves, leading them to view the world in stark extremes. No one really knows how children decide on a mindset, but it is clear that the self-image children construct by elementary school can have an enormous impact on the rest of their lives.

Kids who are praised for being smart, athletic, artistic, or musical tend to develop a "fixed" view, while those who are rewarded or encouraged for their effort in a particular area learn to see ability and character as something that can grow with experience. Children who are overly praised as brilliant or gifted can develop positive self-images, but such labeling can have unintended consequences. Research finds that kids who perceive intellectual ability as fixed tend to underachieve in school because they fear that major challenges will reveal weakness. When faced with difficult tasks, those with fixed views tend to either give up or to cheat. In contrast, children who believe that effort matters are less threatened by setbacks or defeats because they know that it is possible to try harder. Some studies show a correlation between achievement and depression. This can happen when young children view their own self-worth as being dependent on certain qualities—like being smart or being good at sports—even before they learn whether these qualities are innate or acquired. Because young children are unable to distinguish clearly between moral goodness and qualities like beauty, intelligence, diligence, tidiness, and physical ability—these appear all wrapped together for them—this confusion can cause problems for youth whose sense of self-worth depends on their ability to achieve specific goals. In such cases, children who respond with helplessness or despair when a task is too challenging, will only do so if it is in an area they believe matters. For example, a child who sees herself as an athlete might respond to a setback in sports by feeling ashamed and unworthy, whereas one who has decided that her reading and spelling skills make her valuable and not her soccer performance would simply shrug off the same experience. Children with a contingent sense of self-worth—primarily due to parental labeling or coaching—can excel in some tasks while exhibiting symptoms of anxiety, self-hatred, and depression. Such self-images and emotions can lead not only to helplessness and despair but also to desperate need for escape.

While psychological needs and desires drive addiction, these can and do change with time, learning, and development. Physical dependence to drugs does make quitting harder, but if such dependence were the real problem, addiction could be cured simply by waiting out withdrawal. The failure to distinguish between physical dependence and the learning that creates addiction is also why, contrary to claims made in the media, babies cannot actually be "born addicted." Infants can be born with physical dependence on a drug like heroin or Vicodin, but since babies have not learned the vital relationship between choosing to take the drug and feeling better, they do not crave it. Of course, they may feel uncomfortable and distressed if they undergo abrupt withdrawal—but this cannot translate into drug craving, since they don't know what to crave.

Babies' inability to learn the association between getting a drug and feeling better prevents them from developing habitual behavior patterns necessary for addiction. Their early physical dependence may shape their reactions if they take drugs later in life, but this is very different from being "born addicted." Like children of alcoholics and addicts in general, such children are at increased risk for addiction, though the majority will not develop drug problems. For example, while children of alcoholics have a risk of developing alcoholism at a rate two to four times greater than that found in the general population, even if they are adopted by nonalcoholics or raised by parents in recovery, 50 percent do not develop severe drinking problems.[3]

Long before children hit puberty, then, temperament has already started to become established, creating tendencies that can become increasingly difficult to alter. As children learn about their own personalities and how others see them, they create self-concepts and self-worth, further influencing their development. If kids see character as fixed, they may develop a self-defeating perspective; if they see change as possible and achievable, this is less likely. Often, what actually happens in children's lives is less important than how those children interpret their experience. Interpretations made at

3. Ibid., 82.

a young age can promote resilience or increase vulnerability. Such images, like addiction, are learned and shaped by the process of development.[4]

## Generational Personalities

While most individuals can be typed according to traits and personality type, generations in the United States are defined as social groups born around the same time who share similar cultural traits, values, and preferences. Many Americans today readily identify themselves as Boomers, Gen Xers, or Millennials. While a person's birth date may not always be indicative of their generational characteristics, as a common group each generation has similar likes, dislikes, and attributes. Because they share collective experiences, they are said to have similar ideals.

In the US today there are six living generations, which are six fairly distinct groups of people. The following list includes their names, dates of birth, and common attributes.

- The GI Generation, also called The Great Generation (born between 1900–1924). Children of the WWI generation, they experienced the Great Depression and made up the fighting force in WWII. This generational group, entertained by radio and silent movies, is said to be assertive; energetic; team-oriented; community-minded; loyal to jobs, families, and groups; and strong role models.
- The Silent Generation (born between 1925–1945). This group, raised during the Great Depression and WWII, entertained by Big-Band and Swing music, is said to be highly disciplined, self-sacrificing, and cautious. Avid readers with strong intergenerational values and near-absolute truths, the women of this generation stayed home to raise children, men were loyal to jobs and career, and marriage was for life.
- Baby Boomers (born 1946–1964). This generation had two subsets: (a) hippies and save-the-world activists of the 1960s and '70s, and (b) yuppies and social climbers of the 1970s and '80s. The first Rock 'N Roll and television generation, this group is the first to be raised in two-income households. Called the "me" generation for its self-centered views and priorities, this group is said to be optimistic, driven, and team-oriented.

4. Ibid., 83.

- Generation X, also known as Gen Xers (born 1965–1980). This group, the first computer generation, is said to be individualistic, self-reliant, entrepreneurial, short on loyalty, and skeptical. Called "latch-key kids," this group grew up street-smart but isolated, viewing all values as relative.

- Millennials, also known as Generation Y (born 1980–2000). Members of this group, nurtured by "helicopter parents," grew up to believe they were special. Never having known a world without computers, they are digitally literate. Said to be respectful of authority, millennials are known to have high expectations for themselves. Being assertive, with strong views, they are also relaxed and in need of reassurance.

- Centennials, also known as Generation Z or iGen (born 2000–present). This group, known for its cell phone use and dependence on videos, actively promotes personal rights and multiculturalism. Members of this group are said to be savy consumers, knowing what they want and how to get it.

With addiction, it isn't just need or desire that matter as much as set and setting, that is, availability and prevailing cultural norms. For example, while the 1960s and '70s were both periods of individualism, abounding in skepticism and relativism, the 1960s featured sporadic alcohol and marijuana use, relatively mild by comparison with the 1970s and '80s, when widespread use of cocaine resulted in severe and harmful addiction. Early users of heroin, for example, were mostly functional users because the drug's potency was low—3 to 5 percent in the 1960s compared to 40 to 60 percent in the 1980s and beyond. During the 1960s, drug use was counter-cultural, but in the 1970s, drugs were big business, a valuable social currency. By the early '80s, however, greed was acceptable, drugs had become glamorous, and the 1960s-era hippies had transitioned to 1930s-era yuppies. A new generation had emerged, with a new, bold public persona. Cocaine, a drug that makes users feel bold, confident, and on top, suited the age perfectly.

While many people think that drug use peaked in the 1960s and '70s, the new generation, Gen X, proportionally took the most. The late 1970s and early '80s became the heaviest recorded period of illegal drug use by young adults in American history. Among members of Generation X, just under half report having tried cocaine at least once—a remarkable percentage. In 1983, for example, nearly one quarter of college students reported having tried coke at some point, by comparison with the latest figure for undergrads today, which is five percent.

Timothy Leary, the Harvard professor and acid prophet of the Gen Xers, emphasized the importance of what he called "set and setting" as key influences on drug experiences. Set is a person's frame of mind, mood, expectations, and the prevalent cultural ideas about a drug; setting is the physical and social environment in which a substance is taken. Set and setting influence the experience of all addiction and play an important role in whether addiction develops or not. The importance of cultural norms and peer pressures on smoking, alcoholism, drug use, and other addictive substances and behavior, combined with people's needs, states of mind, and expectations, cannot be overestimated. Addiction, as we have stated repeatedly, is not just taking drugs or other harmful substances. It is a pattern of learned behavior that only develops when vulnerable people interact with potentially addictive experiences at the wrong time, in the wrong places, and in the wrong pattern for them.

Despite cultural stereotypes, research finds no universal character traits common to all addicted individuals, and no single addiction personality. Some people, however, seem to be at higher risk for addiction than others, due to set and setting, that is, to specific temperamental traits, parental dysfunction, psychiatric disorders, demeaning labeling, and generational mindset. Nevertheless, the idea of a general addictive personality is fundamentally a myth.

## Questions for Discussion and Reflection

1. In your estimation, is addictive behavior the inevitable outcome of someone's genetic background? Explain your answer.

2. Besides heredity, what additional factors influence the development of someone's personality type?

3. What do we mean by personality "traits," and how do they define one's personality?

4. How are cultural images of addiction misleading?

5. In your estimation, is there such a thing as an "addictive personality"? In other words, do addicted individuals exhibit common character

traits? If so, are these tendencies necessarily antisocial or immoral? Explain your answer.

6.  While it is impossible to connect personality traits with addictive proclivity, can the possession of certain traits or temperamental pathways predispose youth to addiction risk? Explain your answer.

7.  Which functions or regions of the brain must we take into account when examining addictive behavior? Why?

8.  What role can labeling play in promoting addictive patterns and behaviors? Dealing with children and youth, should we avoid labeling altogether, or only use positive labels? Explain your answer.

9.  Assess the idea that babies are "born addicted."

10. Assess the influence of generational personality on one's values, behavior, and self-image. With which living generation do you most identify? Why?

11. How do "set and setting" affect the addictive patterns or behaviors that typify the generation of your birth? Your children's generation?

12. In your estimation, what is the primary insight gained from this chapter?

13. *For personal reflection*: Does this chapter raise any issues you might need to address in the future?

CHAPTER 6

# Addiction and Love

Love is the template for addictive behavior. If your love of a person,
interest, or behavior spurs creativity, connection, and kindness,
it is not an addiction. If a pattern, attitude, or relationship
makes you isolated, dull, and mean, it is an addiction.

—MAIA SZALAVITZ

PEOPLE LOOKING FOR LOVE, whether due to neglect or abandonment by parents, or as the result of failure or rejection in relationships, are at risk of addiction. Surprisingly, people obsessed and driven about relationships, as well as those seeking extreme experience, are also at risk. Since addiction was first described or diagnosed, it has been compared to love. Before compulsive drug use was seen as a disease, it was associated with excessive love. Such correlation was often made by poets and songwriters, who regularly linked sexual passion with desire for particular substances. However, it was not until 1975, when Stanton Peele and Archie Brodsky published *Love and Addiction,* that these passions received a thorough comparative examination. Through meticulous evaluation, the authors illustrated how unhealthy relationships—whether with drugs or with people—share fundamental qualities.

For example, nearly every behavior seen in addiction is found in romantic love.[1] Obsession with the qualities and particulars of the beloved

---

1. The segment on love and addiction is adapted from Szalavitz, *Unbroken Brain,*

84

may be compared with the craving addicted individuals experience if the object of their addiction is unavailable. In some cases, people engage in extreme, uncharacteristic, or even immoral behavior to ensure access. In such cases, withdrawal prompts anxiety and feat; only the drug or loved one can relieve this suffering. Both conditions profoundly alter people's priorities and behavior.

Like addiction, misguided love is a problem of learning. In love, people learn powerful associations between their lovers and nearly everything about them and around them. In addiction, these connections are made with the drug or the compulsive behavior. As visits to certain locations or hearing a specific song can trigger thoughts of a loved one, so certain experiences and memories can spur longing for alcohol or drugs.

In both love and addiction, the stress relief system becomes wired to the object of the addiction, such as needing the drug or the person to feel at ease, in the same way that young children need their parents. In addition, stress often leads to both chemical and romantic relapse. Furthermore, both romantic obsession and addiction rarely appear before adolescence. While both are shaped by life's developmental stages, to really understand how intimately love and addiction are linked, we need to understand how the brain works.

Around the same time *Love and Addiction* was published, research led by Sue Carter at the University of Illinois started to unravel the neurochemistry of what is known in animals as "pair bonding." During these same years, work by Candace Pert and Solomon Snyder in Baltimore led to the discovery of the brain's natural opioids, the endorphins and enkephalins, which are important not only in addiction but in love. "The chemistry of love and addiction turns out to be startlingly similar—both are intimately connected to learning and memory."[2]

Oddly, our understanding of how humans bond chemically began with research on the sex lives of two types of field mice.[3] One, the prairie vole, belongs to the select 5 percent of mammal species that are monogamous, meaning that they form long-term sexual and child-rearing bonds with members of the opposite sex. Another type, known as the montane vole, never commits to a long-term relationship. They mate promiscuously and the males don't parent.

142–47.

2. Ibid., 144.

3. Ibid., 144-45.

When Carter and her colleagues realized that the key difference between these animals was their mating patterns, they recognized that studying their brains could potentially reveal how monogamy is represented anatomically. A study of the voles' brains made these anatomical distinctions clear. The dopamine systems of the two species are wired differently. In female prairie voles, the pleasure and desire circuitry contain large numbers of receptors for the hormone oxytocin. In male prairie voles, this circuitry has receptors for oxytocin but also for the hormone vasopressin. However, in montane voles, both males and females have far fewer of these respective receptors in the relevant regions.

In terms of behavior, this matters significantly. As Carter discovered, oxytocin is critical to the social lives of mammals. Without oxytocin, mice cannot tell friends or family from strangers, and mothers do not learn to nurture their young. Furthermore, the distribution of oxytocin and vasopressin receptors in the pleasure system of prairie voles is what makes them monogamous. The nature and location of these receptors allows the memory of a special partner to be wired into a vole's brain, making him or her the special mate, the one and only partner. This happens during mating, linking the scent of the partner with the pleasure of sex and the comforts of home. Later, when that partner is present, the stress system is calmed and the dopamine and opioid levels rise. In contrast, when the partner is absent, stress rises and withdrawal symptoms ensue. While some prairie voles still "cheat" with other partners, they don't typically leave mates for other "lovers." Montane voles, in contrast, are not wired for monogamy. They don't have enough receptors for oxytocin or vasopressin in their pleasure regions, so they never link the memory of a specific mate with the joys of sex. Sexual novelty, not familiarity, brings pleasure in this species.

Humans seem to be wired like prairie voles. They form pair bonds, but they can also enjoy sexual variety. Studies show that differences in genes for oxytocin and vasopressin receptors play a role in the way humans handle relationships and in conditions that affect social skills. For example, research suggests that variation in the vasopressin receptor gene in men is associated with a 50 percent reduction in the likelihood of marriage and poorer quality marital relationships in those who marry. In both men and women, oxytocin spikes during sexual arousal. This also occurs during childbirth and nursing, and it helps bind parents to their babies. Oxytocin also teaches us who is friendly, or at least familiar, and who is not. Unfortunately, oxytocin can also do the same for one connection to drugs. In such addiction, rather than associating a person with stress relief and pleasure, those connections are made with the drug.[4]

Oxytocin also strengthens social signals and makes them more memorable. While oxytocin on its own does not seem to cause pleasure or desire, it does subtly alter behavior, elevating trust but also hostility. Studies show that it contributes to racism and other types of discrimination, based on whom we see as part of our "in-group" and whom we see as outsiders.

The way oxytocin wires social connections is highly dependent on context, however. In other words, preferences formed in childhood can affect romantic preferences, much like childhood play with peers also affects sexual arousal later in life. In addition, the type of nurturing children receive greatly affects their ability to bond. Having a highly affectionate and responding mother influences certain genes, compared to being raised indifferently. Not surprisingly, neglect and trauma also make social connection more difficult. These changes, too, are mediated by oxytocin, vasopressin, opioids, and dopamine. While chemistry and environment influence how we learn to love and whom we learn to love, changes in chemistry and environment also affect not only how one generation parents its offspring, but also how the next generation will parent and relate to others.

Because oxytocin wiring depends on both genes and the environment, it varies widely. This complexity differs not just between people but it changes within individuals as they form relationships over the course of their development. Since oxytocin wiring addicts us to others, it also plays a critical role in all addictive behavior. Like love, addiction is learned in light of a developmental context. Childhood affects one's risk for addiction in part because of how it affects the way we experience love. This means that each addiction is as individual as each love, making the experience of addiction and the road to recovery immensely variable. "Love really is a drug—or rather, it is the template for addictive behavior."[5]

## Addiction, Love, and Codependency[6]

The idea of codependency—that some people are overly dependent on others and try to escape their own issues by trying to solve other people's problems—is widely accepted and relatively uncontroversial. The stereotype

4. Ibid., 145.
5. Ibid., 147.
6. The segment on codependency is adapted from Szalavitz, ibid., 148–54.

of the wife of an alcoholic who makes excuses for him while trying to convince him to quit does reflect common experience. Such people clearly exist, they are frequently involved with addicts, and it is clear that the "controlling" behavior present when caring people are involved with addicts can be counterproductive.

However, the codependency movement that developed during the 1980s, frequently associated with Al-Anon and the Twelve Step program for family members of alcoholics and other addictive patterns, promoted harmful ideas that persist in addiction treatment and public policy to this day. This movement recognized the link between love and addiction, but in a peculiar and ultimately damaging way. Because addiction was defined as a disease, codependency became one as well.

Moreover, the problem of codependency was soon combined with the idea of "tough love," which diagnosed caring behavior toward people with addiction as "enabling" their addiction to continue. As a result, codependency counselors and Al-Anon members recommended withholding love and material support. Add this to an individualistic culture where any type of dependence on others is seen as weakness and you have a recipe that pathologizes normal human needs while increasing the pain and stigma associated with addiction. Indeed, in the early 1990s some psychologists declared that 94 percent of all relationships were dysfunctional, and a popular cartoon showed a convention for "Adult Children of Normal Parents" as being sparsely attended.[7]

Young people who came of age romantically in the late 1970s and early 1980s had few helpful patterns to follow. The idealism of the 1960s had diminished, divorce had peaked, and leaving spouse and kids to "find oneself" became idealized. Lacking today's awareness of sexual harassment and date rape, there was no cultural template for "dating." The word itself was old-fashioned. Sex was everywhere, but love seemed unattainable, even delusional.

In this context, Peele and Brodsky's *Love and Addiction*, with its strong claim that love is a form of addiction, became a bestseller. However, while the authors' aim was to destigmatize addiction by comparing it to the healthy emotion of love, the cultural setting of the day made addiction seem less pathological while making love seem more so. The book inspired the codependence movement, which saw the book and its message as endorsing their idea of the sickness of people who had relationships with

7. Ibid., 148.

addicts or who were raised by addicts. By the 1990s, the codependency movement grew, fueled by the drug panic of the times and motivated by key figures such as Robin Norwood, author of *Women Who Love Too Much* (1985), and Melody Beattie, who wrote *Codependent No More* (1986). Deep attachment to one's lover became a sign that one had the addictive disease of codependency, and wanting to spend one's time with a single partner was viewed as abnormal and unhealthy. The best way to thwart addiction-like behavior was to end relationships labeled obsessive.

Because the codependency movement was rooted in Twelve Step programs, it was deeply committed to the idea that addiction is a disease. And if addiction was an illness, then codependent love was a medical disorder. The movement grew, despite ignoring the role of learning and culture and how they interact with biology and psychology. "It is a sad irony for us that our work contributed to labeling of yet more 'diseases' over which people are 'powerless,'" wrote Peele and Brodsky in a 1991 preface to an edition of *Love and Addiction*, printed when codependency was the rage. Despite having tried to show that normal love could go awry in compulsive ways—just as drug use can—their work had been interpreted to mean that relationships were addictions, and that love is essentially self-centered and delusional. This logic fit the highly individualized and self-actualized zeitgeist of the 1970s and '80s in America, which denounced racism and sexism while turning self-help into self-love. Some of these ideas were a helpful corrective to inaccurate biological determinism, but they went too far.

We now know that we are fundamentally interdependent—psychologically and physically. Babies, for example, need to be held and cuddled for their stress system to be properly regulated. Without repeated, loving care by the same few people, infants are at high risk for lifelong psychiatric and behavioral problems. During the 1930s and '40s, before this was widely known, one in three infants raised by rotating staff in orphanages died—essentially from lack of individualized love. Their physical needs had been met, but not their emotional ones.

While romantic relationships are not necessary for health, having at least some close relationships is. Research indicates that loneliness can be as dangerous to health as smoking, and more harmful than obesity. In fact, the more and higher-quality relationships a person has, the more mentally and physically healthy they tend to be. Improving relational health improves health in general, for children as well as adults. While it is certainly true that some people behave addictively in their relationships, there is no "codependent" personality, no "brain disease" of codependence, and no predictable course for any such "disorder." "A 'diagnosis' of codependence is about as scientific as a horoscope—and far less entertaining."[8]

Addicted people and those in recovery need loving, positive, relationships. When these are missing, obsessive craving will lead them into unhealthy relationships. Genuine love is the highest and best experience of humanity, and the presence of caring people in the lives of addicted individuals not only help meet unmet needs, but also help them distinguish between good and bad relationships. Love is real when it expands and enhances one's life, and troubling and problematic when it contracts or impairs life. The following rule is helpful: *If your love of a person, interest, or behavior spurs creativity, connection, and kindness, it is not an addiction; if a pattern, attitude, or relationship makes you isolated, dull, and mean, it is an addiction.*[9]

Contrast this with the codependence movement's approach, where passionate love cannot be real love, and where Romeo and Juliet are diseased. More sensible, I believe, is the view that obsessions can get out of hand, but that love, which is inherently obsessive, needs to be that way to bond humans to one another. Nevertheless, obsession alone does not make love an addiction. If all-encompassing passion is itself pathological, then true love is a disease. Love—one of the greatest human sources of joy and meaning—also involves pain and loss, but to demean and dehumanize it is harmful and wrong.

Calling addiction "dependence" subtly implies the same thing. Labeling "caring" as codependence is sexist, for it pathologizes behavior often associated with women. Such labeling faults women (and also devoted husbands) for "loving too much," instead of commending them for upholding human interdependence and for providing relational needs. The problem in addiction is not dependence but compulsive and destructive behavior. If "dependence," is not the real problem in addiction, why pathologize it? Trying to help someone you love, even ineffectually, is admirable, not sick. In fact, the idea that being kind to addicts and "enabling" them does more harm than good is itself damaging. Healthy relationships are essential to recovery, not an impediment. Addicted individuals need more than love, but without it, few will improve. Love may not always cure addictions, but lack of love often prolongs them.

8. Ibid., 151.
9. Ibid., 152.

Of course, determining which relationships are healthy and which are not, and what passion is appropriate and what qualifies as excessive or inappropriate, is not always easy. Human relationships can be messy, and the trade-offs are not always clear. Similarly, applying passion to any activity or behavior, and determining whether it is healthy or dangerously escapist, particularly if it involves danger or risk, is not always simple. Such determinations are ultimately highly subjective, which is why addiction is so difficult to define and address.

Addiction and love are both deeply culturally constructed. This means that they can't be defined generically but rather must be understood when and where they occur. One type and level of drug use may be healthy for one person and unhealthy for another, or even for the same person in a different situation. A glass of wine a day may be healthy in middle age, for instance, but not if you need to take medication that shouldn't be mixed with alcohol. Similarly, passionate attachment that is healthy in one relationship may be harmful in another.

All attachment, ultimately, is shaped by and requires learning. Of course, the learning that occurs in addiction or love is distinct from the way we learn facts about history or science. The role of oxytocin, dopamine, and opioids in wiring future cravings to past memories means that we learn love and addiction more deeply and more permanently than we do things we care less about. Part of the function of emotions is to carve important experiences into memory. Because love and addiction are visceral, these experiences aren't stored like other memories. The changes are deeper, longer lasting, and more pronounced. That's why it is easier to remember our first love than to remember the first time we learned that 2+2=4. "Love and addiction change who we are and what we value—not just what we know."[10]

## Questions for Discussion and Reflection

1.  How is misguided love a problem of learning?
2.  Discuss how "pair bonding" is important not only in love but in addiction.
3.  Explain the chemical and neural connections operant in love.
4.  What roles does oxytocin share in relationships people have with one another and with drugs?

10. Ibid., 154

5. According to this chapter, what is the relationship between love and addiction?

6. How can codependency contribute to alcoholism and other addictive patters, and how can positive, loving relationships be part of the solution to addictive behavior?

7. What does the relationship between love and addiction tell us about successful recovery from addictive patterns and behavior?

8. In your estimation, what is the primary insight gained from this chapter?

9. *For personal reflection*: Does this chapter raise any issues you might need to address in the future?

## CHAPTER 7

# Addiction and Attachment

*Human society shows all the signs of classic addiction.*
—ANNE WILSON SCHAEF

As we conclude our examination of the causes of addiction—associated with traumatic experiences at home, school, and society as well as with personality traits and disorders due to genetics and nurture—we need to consider another source of addiction, America's attachment to wealth and material possessions. Because many of us have more than we need, we should be happy and satisfied. Instead, we seek more, and as a result suffer stress, discontent, and insecurity. The reason is clear: material desires, while not necessarily bad, have a tendency to become addictive because instead of making us whole, they remind us how incomplete, needy, and empty we are.[1]

At this point in human history, we have enough material resources to feed, clothe, shelter, and educate every living individual on earth. Not only that, we have the global capacity to enhance health care, fight major diseases, and considerably clean up the environment. Nonetheless, a quick examination at this warming globe tells us just how far we are from achieving any of these goals. In the past several centuries, the human community has divided into two distinct worlds: a "first" world filled with opulence, luxury, and material excess, and a "third" world characterized by deprivation,

1. Rohr, *Universal Christ*, 87–88.

93

poverty, and struggle. Whereas first and third worlds could formerly be distinguished along national boundaries, increasingly one finds pockets of wealth surrounded by ever widening regions of impoverishment. Most of the world's population is now growing up in winner-take-all economies, where the main goal of individuals is to get whatever they can for themselves. Within this economic landscape, selfishness and materialism are being seen as goals of life.[2]

This global reality exists, however, only because each one of us readily converted to the ideology of consumerism and materialism. Indeed, mass conversion seems already to have occurred. Vast numbers of us are coming to accept the idea that to be well, we first have to be well off. And many of us, unfortunately, are learning to evaluate our identity in terms of our own well-being and accomplishment, not by looking inward at our spirit or integrity, but by looking outward at what we have and what we can buy. Similarly, we have adopted a worldview in which the worth and success of others is judged not by their apparent wisdom, kindness, or community contributions, but in terms of whether they possess the right clothes, the right car, and more generally, the right "stuff."

Perhaps the most insidious aspect of this modern measure of worth is that it is not simply about having enough, but about having more than others do. That is, feelings of personal worth are based on how one's financial resources and possessions compares with that of others. Accordingly, at all levels of wealth one can find individuals who crave gadgets that are ever more expensive, status symbols, and image builders, and who subjectively feel that they need more than they currently have. As advertising executives have known for decades, people become good consumers only when they convert mere "desires" into urgent "needs." By this criterion, most of us have become good consumers.[3]

Are the promises of consumer society true or false? Social institutions, it seems, cannot agree. Wherever we turn, we receive conflicting answers. We can ask the government, but while politicians worry that popular consumer culture has displaced community and family values, economic considerations play a key role in the decisions of most elected officials. We can turn to religious leaders, but while the Bible says that a person who cares about wealth will have trouble entering the kingdom of heaven, some churches, many of them large and new, are pulling in millions of dollars,

2. Richard Ryan's "Foreword" to Kasser, *High Price of Materialism*, ix.
3. Ibid., x.

often to promote elaborate building campaigns and meet the needs of expanding programs and staff.

If we turn to psychology for answers, we find a similar ambivalence about materialistic values. One the one hand, much of the work conducted by evolutionary and behavioral psychologists is compatible with the notion that attainment of wealth and status is of great importance. Similarly, behavioral theories such as those of B. F. Skinner hold that the successful attainment of external rewards is a motivator of all behavior, and indeed fundamental to individuals' adaptation to society. The behaviorist idea that happiness and satisfaction come from attaining wealth and possessions is exemplified by the fact that the founder of American behaviorism, John Watson, took the basic psychological principles of learning and applied them to advertising on Madison Avenue, a model followed by many psychologists.

While behavioral and evolutionary theories largely dominated American academic psychology in the last century, humanistic and existential thinkers such as Carl Rogers, Abraham Maslow, and Erich Fromm voiced a sharply contrasting opinion about materialistic pursuits. Although they acknowledged that some level of material comfort is necessary to provide for basic physical needs, these psychologists suggested that materialistic values can detract from well-being and happiness. Humanistic and existential psychologists place qualities such as authentic self-expression, intimate relationships, and contribution to the community at the core of their notions of psychological health. From this perspective, "a strong focus on materialistic pursuits not only distracts people from experiences conducive to psychological growth and health, but also signals a fundamental alienation from what is truly meaningful."[4]

What does research show? Does money buy happiness? Does affluence make us healthier and better adjusted psychologically? What happens to the quality of our lives when we value materialism?

It would be one thing if the promises of the consumer society were real, but they are not. The formidable body of research into consumerism indicates a surprising and quite counter-intuitive fact, that even when people obtain more money and material goods, they do not become more satisfied with their lives, or more psychologically healthy as a result. More specifically, once people are above the poverty levels of income, gains in wealth have little to no payoff in terms of happiness or well-being. In addition,

4. Kasser, ibid., 2.

according to the research results that Tim Kasser reports in his 2002 *The High Price of Materialism*, merely aspiring to have greater wealth or more material possessions is likely to be associated with increased personal unhappiness. The American dream, it seems, has a dark side, and the pursuit of wealth and possessions might actually be undermining our well-being.[5]

As Kasser shows, people with strong materialistic values and desires report more symptoms of anxiety, are at greater risk for depression, low self-esteem, and problems of intimacy, and experience more frequent physical discomfort than those who are less materialistic. They watch more television, use more alcohol and drugs, and have more impoverished personal relationships. Even in sleep, their dreams seem to be infected with anxiety and distress. And these results are the same for all individuals, regardless of age, income, or culture.

In case one thinks these results only apply to North Americans, it is interesting to note that similar correlations between materialistic values and increased feelings of anger, anxiety, and depression, namely, decreased life satisfaction, have been replicated in samples from around the world, including in England, Denmark, Germany, India, Romania, Russia, South Korea, China, Turkey, Australia, and Singapore.[6]

Another element that these studies measure is narcissistic tendencies. In psychological terms, narcissism describes people who cover an inner feeling of emptiness and questionable self-worth with a grandiose exterior that brags of self-importance. Narcissists are typically vain, expect special treatment from others, and can be manipulative and hostile toward others. Social critics and psychologists often suggest that consumer culture breeds a narcissistic personality by glorifying consumption (for example, "Have it your way," or "You can have it all!").

Recent studies also examine the extent to which materialism is associated with the use of substances such as tobacco, alcohol, and drugs. One study of college students asked how many cigarettes they smoked on a typical day, how often they chewed tobacco, and how often in the last year they had gotten drunk, smoked marijuana, and done hard drugs. When those five indicators were averaged, results showed that young adults with a strong materialistic value orientation are highly likely to use such substances frequently. Unfortunately, these results are confirmed in studies of high school students. Materialistic teens are more likely to engage in

5. Ibid., 9.
6. Ibid., 21–22.

these risk behaviors than are teens focused on other values. In samples of adolescents, college students, and adults, with various means of measuring materialistic values and well-being, results show that the more materialistic values people have, the more their quality of life is diminished. Specifically, these studies show that materialistic values are associated with low self-actualization and well-being, as well as more antisocial behavior and narcissism.

Kasser highlights two reasons why materialism is associated with unhappiness. The first concerns the burdens that materialism places on the human spirit. Desire to have increasingly more material goods drive consumers into an ever more frantic pace of life. Not only must they work harder, but, once possessing goods, they have to maintain, upgrade, replace, insure, and constantly manage them. Rather than controlling possessions, they control us. Thus, in the journey of life, materialists end up carrying an ever-heavier load, one that expends the energy necessary for living, loving, and learning—the really satisfying aspects of that journey. Thus materialism, although promising happiness, actually creates dissatisfaction, and psychological strain.

The second explanation is surprising. If materialism causes unhappiness, unhappiness also "causes" materialism. Enhanced desires or "needs" to consume more are actually deeply connected with feelings of personal insecurity. Materialism, it appears, tends to thrive among people who feel uncertain about matters of love, self-esteem competence, or control. Indeed, to many people materialism appears to offer a solution to these common insecurities and anxieties. Our consumer culture persistently teaches that we can counter unhappiness or insecurity by buying our way to self-esteem and loveworthiness. That's the pervasive message passed on in popular media, that we will feel better about ourselves if we are surrounded by symbols of worth—gadgets that others admire, clothes and adornments that convey attractiveness, or image products that communicate vitality and self-importance. As research indicates, it is because our psychological insecurities are so easily connected with the promise of self-esteem that we keep on consuming.[7]

Remarkably, then, economies focused on consumption appear, in turn, to foster conditions that heighten psychological insecurities, and in this sense they fuel themselves. Children grow up in homes where their parents crave products and possessions. Parents today work more hours

7. Ibid., 28, 52.

outside the home than ever, many to acquire the buying power to obtain more of the goods they have been taught they and their children "need." Meantime, attention to children, intimate time with spouses, and other relationships get pushed to the periphery. Not much for living remains after the working, shopping, and consuming are completed. Yet during this free time, children and adults occupy themselves with mass media crammed with advertisements that entice and promise good feelings ahead. Thus, the cultural climate of consumerism creates the very circumstance where love, control, and esteem are not securely experienced, and in which ever-present self-scrutiny is fostered. In this climate, almost everyone is vulnerable.

If, as evidence show, people strongly oriented to materialistic values are at risk for addiction because they experience low well-being, why is this so? Do materialistic values cause people's problems, or is it the case that people who are already unhappy focus on wealth, possessions, image, and popularity? The answers to these questions are clearly complicated, but they begin with the idea of psychological needs.

Although no one disagrees that all people have certain physical needs (e.g., air, water, food, and shelter) that must be met to ensure survival, some social scientists stop there, saying that psychological needs are either impossible to prove scientifically or do not exist. Some theorists, however, apply the concept of psychological needs to understand human motivation and well-being, and they are supported by substantial research, which suggests that people are highly motivated to feel safe and secure, competent, connected to others, and autonomous and authentically engaged in their behavior. Well-being and quality of life increase when these four sets of needs are satisfied, and decrease when they are not. Materialistic values become prominent in the lives of many individuals who have a history of not having their needs well met. However, materialistic values are not just expressions of unhappiness. Instead, they lead people to organize their lives in ways that do a poor job of satisfying their needs, and thus contribute even more to people's misery.

As noted earlier, the family is the primary socializing environment for most of our early years, and the experiences we have there strongly determine the extent to which we feel safe and secure. The ways parents treat their children, the stability of the family, and the socioeconomic circumstances in which children are raised have important influence in terms of fulfilling needs for safety, sustenance, and security. When family environments poorly satisfy these needs, many children respond by adopting values that emphasize wealth and possessions. Additionally, when mothers were warm, affectionate, and appreciative of their children, whether they imposed many rules and strictures on their children, and how much they allowed their children to express their own opinions and be their own person, also influenced whether teenagers strongly valued financial success or placed more value on self-acceptance, good relationships, or contributed to the community.

While people might assume that greater wealth is associated with greater materialism, studies indicate that teenagers who strongly value materialism are more likely to come from poorer socioeconomic backgrounds than were children who valued self-acceptance, relationships, and community contributions. If growing up in poverty and poor neighborhoods may be partly responsible for creating a materialistic value orientation, this may be due to the fact that such social environments often lead children to feel unsafe and insecure. Unmet needs, then, rather than preexistent wealth, are strong determinants in driving youth to value the materialistic pursuits encouraged by society. Thus, materialistic values can be both a symptom of an underlying insecurity and a coping strategy taken on in an attempt to alleviate problems and satisfy needs.

The problem is that materialistic values are rather poor coping strategies. As with other coping strategies that may make people feel good in the short term (self-isolation, denial of a problem, hedonistic pleasures such as drinking, drugs, and sex), materialistic pursuits may in the long term actually maintain and deepen feelings of insecurity. Negative associations between materialistic values and well-being certainly suggest that such a coping strategy is not especially useful in alleviating people's problems. Like addiction, it probably makes problems worse.

While people generally believe that getting what they want makes them feel good about themselves and their life, evidence suggests that beyond having enough money to meet basic needs, attaining wealth, possessions, and status does not yield long-term increases in happiness or well-being. Even the successful pursuit of materialistic ideals typically turns out to be empty and unsatisfying. Even though Americans earn twice as much in today's dollars as they did in 1957, for example, the proportion of those telling surveyors that they are "very happy" has declined from 35 to 29 percent. Even very rich people report being only slightly happier than average Americans are. Indeed, in most nations the correlation between income and happiness is negligible. Only in the poorest countries, such as Bangladesh and India, is income a measure of emotional well-being. [8]

Self-esteem is understood by most psychologists to be based on people's evaluations of themselves. When people have high self-esteem, they have more positive than negative self-evaluations, feeling good about themselves, and believing they are worthy and valuable. In contrast, people with low self-esteem have more negative than positive evaluations about themselves, felling unworthy, unloved, and inadequate. Many studies have been conducted to understand the role of self-esteem in people's lives, In brief, high self-esteem comes in part from growing up in a warm environment with loving parents and from successfully using one's competencies and abilities to attain one's goals. Low self-esteem occurs when people are neglected and belittled, and when they feel unable to get what they want. This fragile, unstable self-esteem is called "contingent."

Contingent self-esteem clearly shares much in common with how materialistic values are conceived. Values for money, image, and fame cluster together because they all focus on extrinsic concerns. Thus, people with materialistic values hinge their self-esteem and self-worth on whether they have attained some reward (money) or whether other people praise them. Contingent self-esteem is also prominent in one of the psychological problems that occurs with materialistic values, namely, narcissism. Many social critics claim that narcissism is the disorder of our materialistic society, and some theorist note that it often develops as a defense against low self-esteem. According to such views, narcissists attempt to cover feelings of inadequacy by going to the opposite extreme, hiding behind a false sense of worth that is typically dependent on external accomplishments.

Another way in which materialistic individuals may have difficulty in fulfilling their needs for esteem and competence derives from discrepancies. Many psychologists believe that people's emotional states are largely a function of how far they are from where they ideally would like to be. Discrepancies can apply to almost any aspect of people's lives, including their bodies, personalities, and relationships. One person might want straight hair even though hers is curly; perhaps a man wishes he were more outgoing instead of shy; perhaps another wishes she were younger looking; while another wishes he had more hair. Discrepancies can motivate people to engage in beneficial behavior, but if the discrepancy is chronic,

8. This information, reported by psychologists David Myers and Ed Diener, is cited in Kasser, ibid., 3.

or if people feel unable to resolve it, needs for esteem and competence can remain unfulfilled.

While it is natural for people to want to improve their skills, appearance, personality, and intelligence, it is unnatural to pursue these aims obsessively or fanatically, whether through compulsive exercise, cosmetic overuse, sexual enhancements, or recurring liposuction and facelift treatments. While self-improvement is good, perfectionism is not. Ultimately, self-acceptance is essential to happiness, and aging normally and graciously more attractive and healthier than succumbing to Hollywood and Wall Street standards of beauty, success, and well-being.

The ideals that people strive for, and that partly determine discrepancies, come from a number of sources. Personal values are one obvious source, as are societal standards in general. People also develop ideals by looking at the lives of their friends, neighbors, co-workers, and relatives. A great deal of information about what is ideal comes from our culture, particularly through educational, religious, and political systems.

For people oriented toward materialistic values, however, each of these sources can lead to the formation of ideals concerning money, possessions, looks, and status. Several lines of research suggest, however, that these ideals frequently increase one's discrepancies, and thus one's dissatisfaction. And when materialistic ideals romanticize wealth and possessions, to the extent that ideals become unreachable, chronic discrepancies are likely to result. In addition, even if one can reach such ideals, it is not likely to improve one's quality of life. As a result, people may form even higher materialistic ideals, creating new discrepancies and further dissatisfaction. People with strong materialistic orientations are likely to watch a great deal of television, comparing themselves unfavorably with personalities they see there, thereby lowering life satisfaction.

As data show, pursuing materialistic goals, even doing so successfully, fails to increase personal happiness. People may experience temporary improvement of mood, but it is likely to be short-lived and superficial. The sad truth is that when people feel the emptiness of either material success or failure, they often persist in thinking that more will be better, and thus continue to strive for what will never make them happier. In the process, they fail to correct the underlying psychological issues that led them to such an empty pursuit in the first place, and ignore other important psychological needs, such as improving interpersonal relationships and becoming involved in one's community, two cornerstones of personal well-being.

Because values have broad effects on human behavior, the extent to which individuals focus on materialistic pursuits affects the way they interact with other people. When people place a strong emphasis on consuming and buying, earning and spending, and focusing regularly on the monetary worth of things, they likely will treat people like things. Philosopher Martin Buber referred to this interpersonal stance as I-It relationships, in which others' qualities, subjective experience, feelings, and desires are ignored, seen as unimportant, or are viewed only in terms of their usefulness to oneself. In such relationships, other people become reduced to objects, little different from products that may be purchased, used, and discarded. Buber contrasted this objectifying type of relationship with an I-Thou relationship in which other people are recognized as valuable entities in themselves, different from oneself but just as important.[9]

Thus far we have examined three ways in which materialistic values detract from well-being: they maintain deep-rooted feelings of insecurity, they lead to fruitless and never-ending attempts to prove competence, and they interfere with relationships. There is another way in which materialistic values work against need satisfaction and psychological health: they diminish personal freedom. Stated differently, a strong focus on the pursuit of wealth, fame, and image undermines the satisfaction of needs for authenticity and autonomy.

At first, this too seems counterintuitive, for we consider freedom and capitalism to go hand in hand, and consumer goods and personal appearance as primary means by which we express our individual identities. Studies show that individuals who are strongly oriented toward materialistic values place little emphasis on valuing connectedness to others and to their community. A similar value conflict is evident between materialism and autonomy. To the extent that people value wealth, fame, and image, they correspondingly place less value on authenticity and therefore on freedom.

Materialistic values are associated with placing little value on freedom and self-direction, thereby decreasing the likelihood of satisfying these needs. Individuals strongly concerned with materialistic values also enter experiences already focused on obtaining rewards and praise, rather than on enjoying the challenges and inherent pleasures of activities. Furthermore, their values direct them toward activities such as watching television and shopping that rarely provide flow or intrinsic motivation. Finally, materialistic values are associated with the tendency to feel pressured and

9. Kasser, *High Price of Materialism*, 67.

compelled, even in behaviors consistent with these values. Pressure, control, and compulsion, rather than providing paths to freedom and autonomy, make people feel chained and imprisoned. Subtle societal impulses such as these—demeaning, destructive, and addictive—define a life focused on materialistic values.

The struggle against materialism and consumerism rages. Its effects may not be as obvious as the war against opioids and other harmful narcotics, but the results are equally devastating: the loss of soul. The starting point in our battle against rampant consumerism and marketeering is none other than raised consciousness concerning who we are, what we value, and what we strive for in this worldly existence.

## Questions for Discussion and Reflection

1. Assess the concept of attachment as the source or cause of addictive behavior.

2. How can consumerism and attachment to wealth and other material values be a source of addictive patterns and behavior?

3. Are materialism and selfishness connected? Are they "joined at the hip," or merely tangentially related? Explain your answer.

4. What is your idea of the "good life"? How much is sufficient and how do we know when we have enough material belongings and adequate economic security?

5. How are politics, religion, and psychology ambivalent about materialistic values?

6. What critique should we make of our consumer culture?

7. Assess Tim Kasser's conclusions that connect materialistic values with personal unhappiness and decreased life satisfaction.

8. What does this chapter say about the connection between consumerism and narcissism?

9. What does this chapter say about the connection between consumerism and addictive behavior?

10. In your estimation, what is the cause of materialistic values, and what is its antidote?

11. In your estimation, what is the primary insight gained from this chapter?

12. *For personal reflection*: Does this chapter raise any issues you might need to address in the future?

# THE SOLUTION:

## AWARENESS

# CHAPTER 8

# Awareness and Addiction

Addiction to security is the primary cause of insecurity.
—DEEPAK CHOPRA

HAVING ADDRESSED THE NATURE of addiction and its causes, this unit examines the solution to addiction, what we call "awareness," by which we mean self-awareness and self-control, something addicted individuals essentially relinquish.

For generations psychologist thought that virtually all self-defeating behavior was caused by repression. However, addiction is a separate and even more self-defeating force, for it abuses freedom and makes us do things we really do not want to do. While repression stifles desire, addiction attaches desire, bonding and enslaving the energy of desire to certain behaviors, things, or people. These objects of attachment then become preoccupations and obsessions; they come to rule our lives. In this light, we can see why traditional psychotherapy, which is based on the release of repression, has proven ineffective with addictions. It also shows why addiction is the most powerful psychic enemy of humanity's desire for God.

Addiction exists wherever human beings are internally compelled to give energy and priority to things that are not their ultimate desire. A state of compulsion, obsession, or preoccupation that enslaves our will and desire, addiction sidetracks and eclipses the energy of our deepest, truest desire for love and goodness. We succumb because the energy of our desire becomes attached to specific behaviors, objects, or people. Attachment, then, is the process that enslaves desire and creates the state of addiction.

In this sense, we are all addicted. Moreover, our addictions are our own worst enemies. They enslave us with chains that are of our own making and yet that, paradoxically, are quite beyond our control. Addiction also makes idolaters of us all, because it forces us to worship these objects of attachment, thereby preventing us from loving God, ourselves, and one another. Addiction breeds willfulness within us, yet, again paradoxically, it erodes our free will and eats away at our dignity. Addiction, then, it at once an inherent part of our nature and an antagonist of our nature. It is the enemy of human freedom and an antagonist of our nature. Yet, in still another paradox, our addictions can lead us to a deep appreciation of grace, the most transformative force in the universe.[1]

As noted previously, chronically addicted individuals struggle with issues of meaning, identity, and self-worth. Questions such as "Who am I?" and "What is my purpose?" are answered by how individuals handle the challenges of forging a distinct existence across their entire lifespan, from infancy to old age. Navigating the stages of life requires repeated adjustment and accommodation by individuals, particularly as they separate from parents during late adolescence, as they find life partners during early adulthood, determine ways to contribute to society through vocation and parenthood in middle adulthood, and, finally, as they make sense of their life's course in old age.

In life, therefore, people must simultaneously address (1) the limits and possibilities of their particular physical constitution, (2) the limits and possibilities of their own psychological makeup—how they respond to conflict and anxiety and construct meaning out of personal experience—and (3) the limits and possibilities of their particular social contexts—the traditions, expectations, and patterns of their particular family, culture, society, and historical period. The successful navigation of this life journey—determining one's identity—is dependent upon linkage of past, present, and future, upon the contributions of biological, psychological, and social factors at each developmental challenge of life.[2]

Based on this model, how do we understand people trapped in addiction? Since they suffer both the destructive physical and psychological consequences of an addictive existence, their ability to extract meaning from

1. The topic of grace is addressed in chapter 11.

2. Erikson, *Childhood and Society*, cited in Singer, *Message in a Bottle*, 27.

their troubled life or to ward off anxiety without reliance on a substance or behavior is profoundly compromised. Additionally, familial and societal forces undoubtedly contributed to the development of their addiction and now actively aggravate their condition through social ostracism and alienation. In all three aspects of identity—biological, psychological, and social—chronically addicted individuals are scarred. When their condition is exacerbated by poverty, discrimination, inadequate educational resources, lack of health care, and limited access to mental health and counseling services, the climb for those below the line of privilege is formidable. On the other hand, the omnipresence of drugs, crime, and multigenerational unemployment makes the descent below the line of despair attractive and therefore difficult to resist. One individual who repeatedly returned to the drug scene put it like this, "I try to break free, but it feels like the devil has got me by the ankle and won't let go." In many cases, poverty and discrimination are that devil. In such settings, how do chronically addicted individuals address the question of identity?

The first step is up to others in society. Condemnation and dismissal of these people merely compounds the problem. Addicted individuals must certainly be accountable for the damage they have caused and the lives they have harmed, but their accountability does not remove their right to be heard and their needs to be met. Nowhere is this idea better expressed than in the story of the crucifixion in Luke 23:39–43. Two thieves are nailed to crosses next to Jesus. One cries out to Jesus that if he is indeed the Messiah, he should save both them and himself. The other thief cautions the first thief that he should be careful to invoke God, since they have indeed earned their punishment, even if Jesus has not. He then turns to Jesus and, addressing him as "Lord," asks to be remembered when Jesus comes into his kingdom. Jesus answers, "Truly I tell you, today you will be with me in Paradise."

By accepting the consequences of his wrongdoing and acknowledging the possibility of a transcendent world, the thief will join the man he calls his lord in a better world. The message of this passage is a radical challenge. If Jesus, a symbol of goodness and acceptance, shares paradise with a thief, who are we in "normal" society, with our pettiness, vice, and dishonesty, to wash our hands of people in need?[3]

Despite the diversity of factors—sexual, racial, economic, psychological—and the varied nature and level of addiction, those who suffer from

3. Singer. ibid., 126.

chronic addiction experience loss of agency and communion. No longer able to define themselves according to the normative expectations of society, they feel isolated and vulnerable to meaningless and despair. They address this despair through the defensive strategies that precipitate their relapses—surrender of agency, indulgence in harmful habits, and destructive behavior. In so doing, they momentarily dull the pain and loss associated with their lives, even if their disconnection from mainstream society also represents loss of self. What is missing from their identities is the realization that they are embedded in the same world and reality to which the rest of us belong.

The second thief's reply brings us to the second step in the quest for identity. If the problem of addiction is attachment—whether adhering to harmful memories and relations, grasping after temporal material things, or clinging to harmful substances and compulsive habits—the solution is detachment, awareness that allegiance to the ego, to physical substances and behavioral patterns that are merely material and temporal, only produce cycles of guilt and despair. Such allegiance might work in the short term, but it cannot ultimately satisfy our lasting nature. The bottom line, then, is conversion, from patterns of behavior and thought that do not satisfy to patterns that work. The transformation, understood psychologically, is from self-centeredness to self-realization; understood metaphorically, from dreaming to awakening; understood socially, from addiction to awareness; understood religiously, from sin to salvation; understood spiritually, from allegiance to ego to allegiance to grace.

When the spiritual traditions of the world speak of detachment, they describe freedom of desire; not freedom *from* desire, but freedom *of* desire. While this idea could be associated with coldness, austerity, and lack of passion, the association is not valid. Detachment aims at preventing one's self from anxious grasping in order to set the spirit free to love and experience love fully. While detachment requires resolve, it involves more than simply letting go of particular patterns and ideas. The truth is that human beings living out of out of ego gratification and self-sufficiency—out of first-half-of-life-resources—are powerless to enact the transformation required. Changing from first- to second-half-of-life-thinking and living requires unlocking the untapped potential and possibilities underlying the temporary, addicted self.[4] Such transformation is not possible unless it is accompanied by awareness of one's true and eternal self.

4. The preoccupations of the first half of life—self-centric activity such as establishing

Most of us are familiar with the story of the Buddha. Buddhism presents the Buddha (Siddhartha Gautama) as a type rather than as an individual. After his enlightenment, we get no sense of his preferences, dislikes, hopes, or fears. The Buddha, we are told, was trying to find a new way of being human, a way characterized by serenity, equanimity, and profound self-control. While the Buddha's teachings are paradigmatic, equally illustrative are the events that led to his enlightenment.

Buddhist scriptures evolved elaborate mythological accounts of Siddhartha's renunciation of domesticity, including his going forth into homelessness. We are told that when Siddhartha was five days old, his father invited fortunetellers to a feast, where they could examine the infant and foretell his future. The Brahmins concluded that the child had a glorious future: he would become an enlightened spiritual leader or a heroic ruler.

Siddhartha's father, himself a king, deciding his son would become a monarch, confined him to a pleasure-palace existence, insulating him from negative influences or harsh realities. The young Siddhartha lived in delusion, since his vision of the world did not coincide with reality. In his late twenties he experienced a deep discontent with his superficial conditions, which resulted in a complete break with his past. Venturing beyond his confinement, he witnessed four sights that transformed his perspective and his way of life. The "four sights" were of old age, sickness, death, and finally, of a monk whose withdrawal represented detachment from the world. Having opened up to universal suffering, his search for meaning could begin. His quest would not be easy; self-renunciation rarely is.

Renouncing his former life as misguided, Siddhartha set off to find a teacher who could instruct him in the path to enlightenment. During the next three years Siddhartha concentrated fully on his goal. He experimented with many approaches to spirituality, excelling in all but finding them deficient. At first he learned a great deal from his Hindu masters, mastering the essential disciplines, even superseding his teachers in their practice. Before long he concluded that he had learned all that these yogis could teach him. Besides, the teachings remained impractical abstractions, seemingly unrelated to his life. Even his teachers admitted they had not achieved the "direct knowledge" Gautama sought.

---

identity, creating boundary markers, and seeking security—do not constitute the full journey of life. The further journey, which many people never reach, involves soul-centric activity such as acquiring a sense of vision, embracing new urges, letting go of old securities, and risk-taking, particularly willingness to give up patterns of the past for the promise of the future.

He then joined a band of ascetics, following the path of discipline and self-renunciation in order to achieve his goals. But this path only weakened him, resulting in near death. Asceticism proved as fruitless as yoga. But Gautama did not lose hope. He still believed that it was possible for human beings to reach the final liberation of enlightenment. Henceforth he would rely solely on his own insights—and on personal experience. Letting go of cherished dogmas, opinions, and related disciplines, he sat down under an old tree, near a riverbank, where "the beginning of a new solution declared itself to him."[5] Instead of torturing his reluctant self into the final release, he achieved enlightenment in seclusion, effortlessly and spontaneously. It was the moment of his awakening.

What produced this sudden change of perspective, wasn't effort, diligence, or perseverance. Those had proven futile. Gautama had, of course, previously committed himself to the "five prohibitions," moral preliminaries that considered as "unhelpful" activities such as violence, lying, stealing, intoxication, and illicit sex. But now, he realized these were not enough. He must cultivate the positive attitudes that were the opposite of these constraints. Later labeled "The Five Precepts of Buddhism," these behavioral guidelines were believed to encompass the highest form of prayer. *Ahimsa* (nonviolence) could only take one part of the way. Instead of simply avoiding violence, an aspirant must cultivate reverence for life (disinterested compassion), behaving gently and calmly with everything and everyone. It was important not to tell lies, but it was crucial to engage in "right talk," making sure that every word spoken was clear and beneficial. Besides refraining from stealing, individuals should take delight in living simply, cultivating good health by abstaining from intoxicants (by practicing mindful consumption). In Buddhism, abstaining from intoxicants involves refraining from meaningless consumption of food, drugs, or any product that contains toxins, including electronic websites, gambling, television programs, films, literature, even empty conversation.

Once this "skillful means" became habitual, Gautama believed, practitioners would "feel within pure joy," experiencing the divine directly in the present moment, a blissful mental, spiritual, and physical state he later called "nirvana." By resolving to abandon the physical and emotional self-indulgence of his youth and the demanding idealistic path of self-improvement and perfectionism of his young adulthood, the Buddha came to experience for himself what no one else could teach him. "He resolved from

5. Armstrong, *Buddha*, 65.

then on to work with human nature and not to fight against it—amplifying states of mind that were conducive to enlightenment and turning his back on anything that would stunt his potential."[6]

First, as preliminary to meditation, came the practice that he called "mindfulness," living fully in the moment, appreciating its present potential. Initially this meant scrutinizing his behavior at every moment of the day, becoming mindful of his response to any ebb and flow of his feelings and sensations. This practice was not cultivated neurotically, but only as a means to full awareness. The Buddha noted that once distractions were named, they would soon fade away.

Having become convinced that the problem of human suffering lay within himself, mindfulness made him more acutely aware of the pervasiveness both of suffering and the desire that gave rise to it. Awareness of the short duration of his thoughts and longing led to the realization that everything was impermanent. If that were true, he concluded, why cling to objects or to cherished opinions as though they were permanent? This understanding led him to the principle of interbeing and interdependence, based on the unity of all things. If we observe things around us, we find that nothing comes from nothing. Before its so-called birth, a flower already existed in other forms—clouds, sunshine, seed, soil, and other elements. Later on, after its so-called death, the flower's constituents are transformed into other elements, like compost and soil. Interbeing is also interpenetration, because everything contains everything else. Each thing depends on all other things to be. Nothing can exist alone. It has to inter-be with all other things.

Longing for pleasure and permanence are also flawed, the Buddha realized, because they often result in suffering for others. Mindfulness made Gautama highly sensitive to the prevalence of the desire or craving that causes this suffering. Our view of the world, he taught, is distorted by greed, which often leads to ill will and envy. When one's desires clash with the cravings of others, we often find ourselves filled with envy, hatred, and anger. Such states of mind are "unskillful" because they increase our own suffering, selfishness, and discontent.

In the Buddha's system, meditation would take the place of traditional worship, including the place of sacrifice. Likewise, compassion would replace asceticism. Once human beings cultivate friendship for everybody and everything, they can progress to true compassion, empathizing with

6. Ibid., 71.

others in their pain. Finally, humans can attain the state of contemplation, whereby they are so immersed in the object of their contemplation that they are beyond pain or pleasure. Gautama aspired to an attitude of total equanimity toward others, feeling neither attraction nor antipathy. This is a difficult state, since it requires that the practitioner divest completely of egotism, abandoning all personal preference in favor of disinterested benevolence. In his enlightenment, Gautama learned "to transcend himself in an act of total compassion toward all other beings, infusing the old disciplines with loving-kindness."[7]

If there is any truth to the story that Gautama gained enlightenment under the Bodhi tree, it could be that he acquired a sudden, absolute certainty that he had discovered a method that would bring an earnest seeker to nirvana. He never insisted that his method was new or an invention of his own. Rather he noted that he had simply discovered an ancient path that elucidated the fundamental principles that govern the life of the cosmos. His path was simply a statement of things "as they really are," a way written into the very structure of existence. If living beings kept to the path of interdependence, they could attain a state that would bring them peace and fulfillment, because they no longer struggled against one another or their deepest grain.[8] When the Buddha achieved nirvana under the Bodhi tree, he did not shout "I am liberated," but "It is liberated." Having conquered the fires of greed, hatred, and delusion, he awakened to his full potential as a human being. He had found an inner realm of calm, thereby becoming a Buddha. He was no longer asleep, but awake, no longer deceived, but aware.

In his public lecture "The Seven Spiritual Laws of Success," the prominent Indian-American physician and philosopher Deepak Chopra defines success as "the progressive realization of worthy goals." Humans are goal-seeking organisms. Because worthy goals involve the ability to love and be compassionate, harmful addictive behavior qualifies as unworthy. From this perspective, a requisite quality for goal seeking is the ability to hear one's inner voice, to be in touch with the Spirit within, one's true self and creative center. Living out of one's core, one's innermost being, Chopra believes, is what humans mean by "spirituality."[9] Spirituality, simply defined, is "Self-

7. Ibid., 78.

8. Ibid., 82–83.

9. Since not all of Deepak Chopra's "Seven Spiritual Laws of Success" apply to our discussion, I mention a complete list here solely for the reader's benefit: 1. The Law of Pure Spirituality or Pure Potentiality. 2. The Law of Giving and Receiving. 3. The Law of Karma (of Cause and Effect). 4. The Law of Least Effort. 5. The Law of Intention and

awareness." You will notice I have capitalized the word "Self," for this is both intentional and essential to a proper understanding of the concept.

Because it is easy to fall into a simplistic or merely humanistic view of spirituality, let me clarify what I mean. When I think of spirituality, I have in mind the account of Jesus healing blindness in Mark's Gospel. According to Mark 8:22–26, when Jesus healed a blind man in the town of Bethsaida, the healing occurred in three stages. First, the man was blind. Next, Jesus laid hands on him, using saliva to anoint the man's eyes. However, the man's vision was blurry and indistinct. Lastly, Jesus again laid hands upon the blind man's eyes, whereupon his sight was fully restored, enabling him to see everything clearly.

The same pattern can be applied to spirituality (its three stages also understood as three distinct types of spirituality):

1.  *self-consciousness.* This stage of awareness—the first-half-of-life-phase—denotes "self-awareness," a selfish, self-centered, egocentric state. Characterized by allegiance to the ego or false self, this stage represents deception and spiritual idolatry. In this stage, a false and dream-like state, humans are in the dark, unaware, and self-deceived.

2.  *God-consciousness.* This phase, a transitional phase, is still idolatry, or, more accurately, monolatry, for as commonly understood, it represents institutional allegiance, attachment to ethical and man-made religious belief systems. This phase of spirituality, evident historically in salvation by effort approaches, can be likened to sleep-walking. In this stage participants are striving to make progress, but they are still in the dark. They are serving external requirements, pleasing an authoritarian deity.

3.  *Self-consciousness.* This phase, one of awareness, is entered through realization, by awakening. Those thus connected to their soul or core being are now "in the light," connected finally to their higher power, to pure consciousness. Such awareness—such living and thinking—are gifts of grace. This state of awareness cannot be earned, but, like the biblical pearl of great price, it can be found through diligent search and desire.

These stages represent the journey from darkness to light, illustrated in nature by the three phases of the twenty-four-hour day: night, twilight/

---

Desire. 6. The Law of Detachment (or Non-Attachment). 7. The Law of Dharma (or Purpose in Life).

dawn, and day. To clarify what I mean by these three stages or types of spirituality, allow me to illustrate by means of a crass analogy. I am a fan of certain reality shows on television, particularly "Survivor" and "The Bachelor-Bachelorette." Even though there is a great deal to criticize in the latter show, I believe that for the majority of participants, the situation is quite real: they are sincerely searching for love! The method for doing so, however, is often vulgar and hedonistic. The show follows a specific pattern, consisting of three phases. In phase 1, the bachelor or bachelorette dates twenty-five or more eligible suitors. This phase, like the "self-conscious-ness" phase of spirituality, can be glamorous but also superficial and filled with drama. Phase 2 comes near the end of the show, when the bachelor/bachelorette falls in love, usually with more than one suitor. This phase, involving hometown visitations and fantasy suites, can be helpful, while also filled with anguish and uncertainty. During phase 3 the field of suitors is narrowed to one, ending in engagement or proposal of marriage.

The process is predictable, except during the 2019 show, when the current bachelor, Colton, found himself falling in love with three suitors, two of whom expressed their love in return. However, during the home-town visits, Colton failed to secure the "blessing" of Cassie's father, and she, in turn, was unable to commit to Colton, even after he declared his love for her alone. Colton, however, "all in," was already in phase 3 of his commit-ment. Anxious and desperate when his declaration of love was spurned by Cassie, Colton jumped an eight-foot gate and headed off into the Portu-guese countryside, seemingly abandoning the show. Though he eventually returned, he relinquished control of his future, including the sure love of two worthy candidates, by risking his future on Cassie. Forsaking all guar-antees, he willingly took a chance on love. In the end, Colton won Cassie's heart, their goals united and fulfilled.

Returning to our discussion, it is important to understand that whatever ultimate reality we experience in "Self-consciousness" cannot be gained solely through self-effort, else it would be phase-1 activity. To experience Self-consciousness is to align with the cosmic power already present within. When we put Chopra's first law into effect, *the Law of Pure Potentiality* (or Pure Spirituality), what is latent and invisible in the universe becomes manifest in our lives. To become manifesters, however, humans need to practice awareness, a transformative mindset akin to re-ceiving a heart and mind transplant. To enter this phase requires using a key we already possess.

In his groundbreaking text, *The World's Religions* (originally published in 1958), Huston Smith begins the chapter on Hinduism with an intriguing statement: "If we were to take Hinduism as a whole—its vast literature, its complicated rituals, its sprawling folkways, its opulent art—and compress it into a single affirmation, we would find it saying: "You can have what you want."[10] However, after discussing what people want—pleasure, worldly success, moral attainment, and liberation (by which he means something akin to fulfillment, transcendence, or infinite bliss)—Smith states that these goals, while startling, are not only within our reach, but that we already possess them. In other words, what we want, we already have. If this is true, why is it not apparent, and why do we not act accordingly? The answer, according to the spiritual traditions, is that the eternal is buried under an almost impenetrable mass of distractions, false assumptions, and self-regarding instincts that comprise our surface (false) selves.

Having examined the Law of Pure Spirituality, let us consider three additional spiritual laws, Chopra's Law of Detachment (or Non-Attachment), the Law of Cause and Effect, and the Law of Purpose in Life. *The Law of Detachment* addresses the craving, grasping, and clinging that characterize all addictive behavior. Addicted individuals seek attachment, whether to a substance, a person, or a specific behavior. Fixed or deterministic systems spurn creativity, but detachment represents freedom and uncertainty, which in turn allows for creativity. In *Breathing under Water*, his book on alcoholism and the Twelve Step program, Franciscan friar Richard Rohr agrees with Chopra, building upon Paul's use of the terms "flesh" (ego) and "spirit" or soul. The ego self, lacking inner substance, is defined by attachments and revulsions, whereas the soul is free of attachments; its desire centered on letting go. Rohr uses incarnational theology (see Phil. 2:7) to illustrate that the spiritual journey to find God is less about trying to get "up there" than about acknowledging that in Christ, God is already "down here" with us. Ironically, much religious worship and effort is the spiritual equivalent of "trying to go up what has become the down elevator."[11] Because in Christ, God is forever overcoming the gap between human and divine, the real spiritual journey is less about climbing and performing and more about descending, letting go, and unlearning. For Rohr, all mature spirituality is about detachment. The soul neither attaches, nor hates; it only loves and

---

10. Smith, *The World's Religions*, 13.
11. Rohr, *Universal Christ*, 110.

lets go. As the German mystic Meister Eckhart stated, the spiritual life has more to do with subtraction that with addition.[12]

In detachment lies freedom from our past, from what we call "the known." The known is simply the prison of past condition. While most human beings—certainly addicted individuals—seek to live in the known, in the environments they find meaningful and rewarding, the fact is that everything beyond the present moment is unknown. Therefore, if our intention is to leave the securities and patterns of the past and head in new directions, we must enter the unknown, the realm of infinite possibilities. When we surrender cherished lifestyles and opinions, we yield to the creative mind that orchestrates the universe. Embracing stage 3 spirituality breaks the bonds of addiction and empowers transformation, from self-consciousness to Self-consciousness, from false worship to true worship.

How do we apply the Law of Detachment? According to Chopra, we put it into effect by making a commitment to the following steps:

1.  Today, I will commit myself to detachment. I will allow myself and those around me the freedom to be as they are. I will not rigidly impose my idea of how things should be. I will not force solutions to problems, thereby creating new problems. I will participate in everything with detached involvement, engaged—even passionately so—and yet detached at the same time.

2.  Today I will find security in the wisdom of uncertainty. I will factor uncertainty as an essential ingredient of experience. And in my willingness to accept uncertainty, solutions will emerge. Out of confusion, disorder, and chaos, creative solutions will emerge. The more uncertain things seem, the more secure I will feel, because uncertainty is my path to freedom.

3.  Today, I will step into the field of possibility. I will anticipate the excitement that can occur when I remain open to new choices. Today I will experience all the fun, the magic, and the mystery of life, free from compulsion and consumerism.

According to *the Law of Cause and Effect*, all behavior has consequences. Every action releases energy that returns in like kind, like an echo from the past. How do we apply this law? We put it into effect by making a commitment to the following steps:

12. Rohr, *Breathing under Water*, 5–6.

1. Today, I will be mindful of the choices I make. By witnessing these choices, I will bring them to conscious awareness. I will affirm that the best way to prepare for the future is to be fully intentional in the present. When I make a decision, I will ask, "What are the consequences of my decision?" "Will this choice bring fulfillment and happiness to me and to all others affected by my action?"

2. Today, I will ask my heart (your heart knows better than your mind), "What do I really need?" If your choice makes you comfortable, then proceed boldly. However, if the choice feels uncomfortable, then pause and consider the consequences of your decision. The guidance you receive from your heart will enable you to make spontaneously beneficial choices for yourself and for those around you. Why is it important to examine your inner will and consciousness? Because they are related to the infinite real of reality, and hence to cosmic meaning and purpose. Connecting the finite to the infinite makes the invisible visible. When this transfer of consciousness and energy occurs, we discover who we are, what we want, and our life's purpose.

3. Today, I will take responsibility for situations and events I see as problems. Accepting responsibility does not mean blaming myself or others for my problems, however, for blame only produces guilt and shame. Responsibility means "response ability," that is, "ability to respond." Therefore, the more aware we are in our responses, the more creative we can be of the potential latent in every moment. The Law of Cause and Effect allows us to view problems as opportunities in disguise. Alertness to opportunities—considering problems as challenges—helps turn them into opportunities.

The best way to understand our final principle, *the Law of Purpose,* is to acknowledge that every person has a purpose, a unique gift, or a special talent to give to others. How do we discover this talent? A good way to do so is to ask oneself the question, "What if I had all the money in the world, and all the time in the world, what would I do with them?" Having answered this question, how would you express this gift, and who would benefit? The answers are a clue to what your unique skills are. When people express their unique talent in service to others, they experience the exaltation of their inner spirit. Ultimately, that is the goal of experience, to exalt in one's spirit. Joy, happiness, fulfillment—these are the goals of the universe, and our goals as well. All people are born with the unique ability both to identify their unique skills and talents and to express them in service to others. A good image of the universe is that of a jigsaw puzzle, where each piece belongs and is necessary.

How do we apply the Law of Purpose? By making a commitment to the following steps:

1. Today, I will nurture the divine spark of the infinite that animates my heart, mind, and body. Today I will awaken to the deep stillness within, carrying the consciousness of eternal being in my time-bound experience.

2. Today, I will make a list of my unique talents, including all the things I love to do while expressing these abilities. After making this list, I will learn I am using my abilities wisely, that is, in the service of others, when I lose track of them. In the process, I will discover that putting my gifts into effect is no longer work but play, no longer difficult but effortless. Through that discovery, I will create abundance for myself as well as for others.

3. Today, I will ask myself four questions, their answers percolating naturally and effortlessly from my creative core, my spiritual center: (a) "Who am I?" or "What am I?" (b) "What do I want?" or "What is my deepest desire?" (c) "What is my purpose?" or "How can I serve, how can I help?" and (d) "For what am I grateful?"

The answers to these questions, in the context of stage 3 spirituality, will open the door to spiritual success and abundance. How we answer these questions, and the degree to which we are committed to the further journey—this second-half-of-living mindset—determines our current state of spirituality. When we experience that part of us that is formless and invisible, and accept it as truth, this is transcendence, the holiest of experiences. With transcendence comes goodness, beauty, harmony, and spontaneity. When we see these in an object, we experience it as beautiful. When we see them in another person, we experience it as love.

## Questions for Discussion and Reflection

1. What does the author mean by awareness, and why is awareness important in our struggle with addiction?

2. What does the author mean when he equates addiction with idolatry? What, according to this chapter, is humanity's ultimate goal or desire, and how does addiction prevent us from attaining that goal?

3. This chapter introduces the concept of grace, calling it "the most transformative force in the universe." Although grace is central to ensuing chapters, it might be helpful at this stage to construct a personal or group definition (if appropriate) of grace. What do we mean by grace, and how is it important to recovery from addiction?

4. What does the author mean by "establishing identity," and how is establishing identity significant for people trapped in addiction?

5. What does the account of the two thieves crucified with Jesus teach us about helping people trapped in addiction?

6. How does the story of the Buddha illustrate the concept of awareness?

7. Explain the three stages or phases of spirituality. How can spirituality (understood as "Self-awareness") help to free us from harmful addictive behavior and to attain "worthy goals"?

8. Assess the merits of Huston Smith's enigmatic notion, "what you want, you already possess."

9. Assess Deepak Chopra's Law of Detachment. How can you apply this law to your life?

10. Assess Chopra's Law of Cause and Effect. How can you apply this law to your life?

11. Assess Chopra's Law of Purpose. How can you apply this law to your life?

12. In your estimation, what is the primary insight gained from this chapter?

13. *For personal reflection:* Does this chapter raise any issues you might need to address in the future?

# CHAPTER 9

# Awareness and Power

Whenever I am weak, then I am strong (2 Corinthians 12:10).
I can do all things through [Christ] who strengthens me (Philippians 4:13).
—PAUL OF TARSUS

UNDERLYING ALL ADDICTION ARE the misuse of power and failure to re-linquish control. Wealth, like all material objects, can be addictive; like-wise pornography, drugs, gambling, sports, smoking, entertainment, and pleasure. Even religion can be addictive. When temporal entities—and the realms they represent—promise humans abilities and qualities they cannot deliver, such as wealth, happiness, freedom, escape, and fulfillment, they become idols, false gods. This is so because they seek allegiance, promising human mortals qualities they inherently lack—self-fulfillment, self-real-ization, and self-satisfaction. These false gods are the "powers and princi-palities" about which believers are warned in the New Testament, termed "cosmic powers of this present darkness" and "spiritual forces of evil" by the author of Ephesians. Ephesians 6:11–17 depicts the warfare of God's people against false powers. Seduced and tempted by the flaming arrows of evil, believers are exhorted to defeat evil by taking on the "whole armor of God," including the belt of truth, the breastplate of righteousness, the shield of faith, and the sword of the Spirit.

The powers of evil are real, as Jesus discovered in the wilderness of Judea and throughout his life, their guarantees formidable—material prosperity, physical prowess, charismatic appeal, political influence (see Luke 4:1–13). While Jesus was offered ultimate authority in exchange for his soul, the powers of evil initially ask of us only minimal allegiance, merely a pound of flesh. For most humans, however, defeat is a matter of time. We succumb because we are inherently weak and incurably turned inward, seeking domination and control over others, circumstances, material objects (which we call "possessions" when they are acquired), and ourselves. We seek control because we have been taught that control brings happiness and success. In actuality, the reverse is true. As spiritual masters indicate, only non-attachment—letting go of control—brings happiness, fulfillment, and peace, because through detachment comes release from fear, stress, insecurity, unhappiness, and lack of fulfillment. When we are weak, the apostle Paul discovered, we are strong.

As psychotherapist Anne Wilson Schaef notes, human society shows all the signs of classic addiction. As we are unable to stop sea levels from rising or prevent other effects of global warming, so we are powerless to stop the waters of our addictive culture from rising. Ignorance, however, is not bliss. If faith can move mountains, one individual can make a difference, and a group of likeminded individuals can change the world. It happened before, and it can happen again.

## Powerlessness

Essential to the Twelve Step model of recovery is the concept of "hitting bottom." That concept originated with Alcoholics Anonymous in 1935, when Bill Wilson, newly dry and having had a religious awakening, met physician Bob Smith, a particularly tough case. Within six hours, however, Bill had convinced Bob to try sobriety, and that meeting forever changed the way America saw addiction. Both A.A. founders had lost a great deal to alcohol before they created the program. Most of A.A.'s earliest members were what the program labeled "low bottom" drunks, some of whom had literally been on skid row and fallen as far as possible socially and emotionally, without dying. One of the group's foundational texts, *12 Steps and 12 Traditions*, affirms that recovery cannot begin unless an addicted person first feels completely defeated, admitting "powerlessness" over alcohol.

Bill W., as he is known, was a successful stockbroker, married and at one point prosperous, who drank himself into endless job changes, debt, and repeated hospitalization. Roller-coast periods of sobriety and times of temptation eventually led him to a spiritual fellowship called the Oxford Group and to Dr. Bob, notorious for his alcoholism. Eventually Bill W. and Dr. Bob joined forces and the self-help movement known as Alcoholics Anonymous was born, a fellowship of individuals suffering from a common affliction, who through reliance on God and shared understanding helped bring one another back to sobriety.

Over the next sixty years, a narrative of addiction and recovery developed. Inspirational accounts of early members are recounted in A.A.'s *Big Book*, including those of Bill Wilson and Bob Smith. While each story is unique, general aspects of the early narrative can be identified. Often suffering devastating loss in life—possibly including job, marriage, custody of children, standing in the community, and self-respect—the recovering alcoholic reaches bottom and seeks help. Through recovering individuals, counselors, clergy, hospitals, law enforcement officials, or loyal family members, addicted individuals eventually connect with A.A. programs, where they learn to accept powerlessness over addiction. Over time, groups such as Narcotics Anonymous, Cocaine Anonymous, and other Twelve Step programs emerged, rewriting A.A.'s steps and literature to substitute their problem drugs or activities for alcohol. In 1951, Bill Wilson's wife, Lois, cofounded Al-Anon, an independent support group for relatives and friends of alcoholics.

People in recovery are expected to share their story and listen to others' stories of how alcohol or drugs devastated their lives.[1] They are also encouraged to turn their lives over to a higher power (however individually imagined or expressed), and to rely upon prayer and peer fellowship to guide their recovery. In addition, Twelve Step programs include self-reflection, self-disclosure, making amends, and assisting those seeking sobriety. Over time, addicted individuals regain their sense of self-respect and the trust of loved ones. Strengthened by Twelve Step recovery programs, addicted people return to homes and career and strive to regain economic security. The road to sobriety involves transformation of life, which includes gaining spiritual meaning that may have been lacking during active alcoholic or drug-using periods.

---

1. In this regard, readers may want to hear one or more of the thousands of stories dramatically narrated in the *Unshackled* radio series, thirty-minute evangelistic programs featuring the account of someone freed from alcoholism through conversion to Christ. This dramatic series, originally produced by Pacific Garden Mission in Chicago, Illinois in 1950 and now available on YouTube, is one of the longest running radio programs in history.

Most people who enter Twelve Step programs feel they have "hit bottom." They have discovered, over time, that their willpower and self-control over alcohol or other drugs have become practically nonexistent. They are desperate, wanting to stop but unable to do so.[2] For years they believed the lie that they were like other people, able to control their behavior. The first step in their recovery was being honest with themselves, confronting delusions they had created, distortions of mind and body. That discovery, that they are bankrupt physically, mentally, emotionally, and spiritually, is the first step in recovery.

While acknowledging powerlessness over alcohol or drug abuse is essential to recovery, the concept of "bottom" is subjective. In addition, "hitting bottom" can only be defined retrospectively, after recovery. If people relapse—and at least 90 percent of addicts relapse at least once—then by definition they have not yet hit bottom.[3] How low must they go before they hit bottom? And what if there is a trapdoor lower still? Research shows that recovery differs widely from one addict to another, and from one addiction to another. While some people bounce back easily after a relapse, others get worse, and yet others enter a static cycle of recovery and relapse, getting neither worse nor better. Tragically, some also die.

While the Twelve Step approach has changed lives around the world, it does not work for everyone—on average, 70 percent of those referred to A.A. drop out within six months[4]—and when applied by secular treatment centers or by law enforcement programs, the method can be distorted.[5] Working with chronically addicted individuals, clinical psychologist Jefferson Singer discovered that the Twelve Step model assumes a certain approach to identity formation that many of his patients could never attain. For example, it seems to work better for people who are comfortable with group meetings and who accept societal values. Furthermore, treatment

2. Alcoholics liken alcohol cravings to diarrhea; willpower alone cannot stop them.

3. Szalavitz, *Unbroken Brain*, 183.

4. Statistics, of course, can be misleading. Of those who leave A.A. or relapse, many return, finding sobriety over time.

5. Szalavitz, *Unbroken Brain*, 218. Szalavitz is one of many who question the validity of A.A.'s concept of powerlessness, believing that focus on powerlessness can make things worse. While the disease model and the concept of powerlessness can lead to externalizing blame and abdicating responsibility, this is not how Twelve Step programs work. Coupled with powerlessness is acceptance of responsibility. Only through contrition, including admission of poor choices and irresponsible behavior—"I am an alcoholic; I am an addict, and I need help"—can there be hope of recovery.

centers and law enforcement officials who recommend the Twelve Step format are now asking programs to respond to levels of social dysfunction and psychopathology they had not encountered previously and were not intended to address.

While Alcoholics Anonymous offers a solid foundation and scaffolding for recovery from alcoholism—that is its singleness of purpose—some individuals in recovery face interior work of such complexity that they are unable to recover by the guidance of A.A. alone. In addition to chronically mentally ill addicts and cross-addicted abusers, people with long-standing psychological conflicts often find that Twelve Step programs alone are not sufficient to achieve a sustainable recovery. As we have indicated, chronic drinking or drugging problems may have begun as efforts to repress and escape recurrent memories of trauma or abuse. Sexual, physical, and psychological abuse of both females and males may be a factor, and individuals with firsthand exposure to violence or unexpected death, such as combat veterans, parents who have lost a child, and survivors of accidents or street violence, may present treatment demands that go beyond mere referral to Twelve Step programs. Similarly, individuals struggling with sexual identity and societal homophobia, men with sexual desires for children, and people with sexual compulsions or fetishes, should not attend Twelve Step meetings expecting treatment. The Twelve Step format is not an appropriate forum for working out such conflicts and confusions.

For people with phobias and personality disorders, going to meetings might lead to nausea, hyperventilation, or self-consciousness bordering on psychosis. Furthermore, emotionally shallow narcissistic individuals might dominate a meeting with tales of personal triumphs or tragic failures, finding little benefit in listening to others. Additionally, some individuals may be unable to let go of their secrets and face the consequences of public self-disclosure. Though Twelve Step programs contain much wisdom in their message and approach, people with chronic mental illnesses, cross-addictions, or long-standing psychological conflicts, should not be referred to these organizations.

In chapter 8 we learned the story of the Buddha. However, we did not mention the Buddha's most famous teaching, his approach to the problem of life captured in the Four Noble Truths. The Buddha's approach, like that of A.A., is essentially that of a physician. The Buddha began by examining carefully the symptoms that provoke concern. If everything went smoothly in life, there would be nothing about which to worry or be concerned.

However, this is not the case. There is more pain, fear, resentment, stress, failure, and conflict than we believe should exist. These *symptoms* the Buddha summarized in the First Noble Truth: "All life is suffering." The Second Noble Truth was *diagnosis*: "The cause of suffering is desire" (addiction?). The *prognosis*, summarized in the Third Noble Truth, is hopeful: "There is a cure for desire (addiction)." This brings us to *prescription*, how overcoming desire (addiction) is accomplished. The Fourth Noble Truth provides the answer: "The cure for desire is through the Eightfold Path." The Eightfold Path, like A.A.'s Twelve Steps, is a course of treatment.[6] Buddhism's Eight Steps consist of attaining Right Views, Right Intent, Right Speech, Right Conduct, Right Livelihood, Right Effort, Right Mindfulness, and Right Concentration.

The Buddha's methodology, accepted by people around the world, is relevant to our understanding of the Twelve Step approach to addiction. The genius of Twelve Step programs is that they combine the monotheism of Western religious traditions with the methodology of the Eastern religious traditions. The message of Alcoholics Anonymous, as encapsulated in the Twelve Steps, unites Eastern and Western approaches to the journey of life and life's problems in a remarkable way, something that explains AA's success globally.

## The Potential Misuse of Power by Secular Treatment Centers

In 1935, when Bill Wilson and Dr. Bob Smith created A.A., both were members of the Oxford Group, a Christian revival movement. They based the twelve steps on the group's principles of surrender to God, self-awareness, restitution for harm done, prayer, and proselytism. Shortly thereafter, A.A. split from the Oxford Group, intent on becoming more ecumenical.

Soon medical professionals—from detox doctors and nurses to rehab physicians and counselor—began viewing addiction as a medical disease, and the prescribed treatment was meetings, moral inventory, and prayer, substituting religion for actual medicine. Despite this contradiction, Twelve Step programs offer hope—the "power of example"—and for many people, it works. As research shows, social support aids recovery and is essential for mental and physical health. Love may not be a cure-all, but without love, psychological and learning disorders are practically incurable.

6. Smith, *The World's Religions*, 104.

When alcoholics join A.A., the first step—admission of powerlessness over alcohol—seems obvious. The second and third steps—belief in a higher power and accepting help from this power, while a problem for atheists, agnostics, and skeptics, are also indispensable. The remaining steps, beginning with the fourth and fifth—taking a fearless moral inventory of oneself and disclosing this list to another person—are also essential in defeating addiction.[7] While listing one's faults, fears, and resentments can be manipulated or used maliciously by hostile individuals, as in confrontational treatment settings, introspective honesty can be the first step in one's liberation. Viewing behavior and character as malleable can also provide addicted individuals hope of change and expectation of progress.

Significantly, when people are *forced* into Twelve Step programs, they do no better—and sometimes worse—than when given alternatives or no treatment. One study of over two hundred workers mandated by their employers to get help and randomized to Twelve Step programs, hospital-based treatment, or a choice of treatment, showed the mandated group fared worse, 63 percent requiring additional treatment compared to 38 percent for the choice group and 23 percent for the hospital group.[8] I am not saying that the Twelve Step method is useless, for it produces outstanding results for those who attend voluntarily and connect with a sponsor. The fact that these programs are free and available worldwide makes them a tremendous resource for an underfunded, stigmatized area of health care that will remain at risk for the foreseeable future.

As a Depression-era organization, Alcoholics Anonymous took off, its impact spontaneous and formidable. Soon the notion of the need to hit bottom became popular with treatment providers, who began basing their treatment on the twelve steps with the founding of Hazelden in Minnesota in 1949. By 2000, 90 percent of all addiction treatment was twelve-step based. As A.A. grew, celebrities added to its membership, making rehab appear almost glamorous. Not coincidentally, the idea that addicts need to hit bottom before they can recover also suited the punitive approach America takes with drugs.

While A.A's program is effective in recovery from addiction, it is not relevant in medical or secular settings. Imagine a psychiatrist telling a

---

7. Building a mind, like building a soul, is a lifetime endeavor. Step Four is the beginning of a lifetime practice. Readers wishing to put this step into practice are encouraged to examine appendix B.

8. Szalavitz, *Unbroken Brain*, 217–18.

depressed person to surrender to God and to take a moral inventory. Better yet, imagine a doctor proposing this treatment to someone with cancer or AIDS. Imagine group therapy for autism or attention deficit disorders putting individuals on a "hot seat," where patients try to break others down through humiliation and listing flaws in their personality. Unfortunately, these tactics were common in addiction treatment during the second half of the twentieth century, after word of A.A. spread, including a 1941 article in the *Saturday Evening Post* magazine that quadrupled membership in A.A. within a year. As a result, members and medical professionals began to import its ideas into treatment settings like hospitals. They also created residential center for A.A. members who needed intensive support. And this is where the trouble with the idea of "bottom" began. Hazelden's "Minnesota Model" became the template for the 28-day inpatient rehab and for most outpatient treatment. Although today these programs are typically gentle and work through persuasion, many went through a period when humiliation and emotional attacks on patients seemed acceptable ways to shove them downward. The use of humiliation and "attack therapy" culminated at Synanon, a commune started in 1958.

Synanon's founder, Chuck Dederich, decided that A.A. was too soft on alcoholics and addicts. He conducted therapy groups during which members played what became known as "the Game," persisting for hours, even days, without breaks. The idea was to break a person's ego, using secrets people revealed to obliterate the "character defects" believed to characterize all people with addiction. By the late 1960s, Synanon had won national acclaim, and state officials across the country sent representatives to study it and create local programs. Only one state, New Jersey, bothered to evaluate Synanon before replicating it, discovering that the vast majority of participants dropped out within a few weeks and that only about 15 percent stayed abstinent. While Synanon did not duplicate the twelve steps, it distorted the idea of powerlessness, introducing the idea of breaking people to achieve bottom.

While the Twelve Step approach is helpful when freely chosen, it can be harmful when it involves coercion, particularly when hitting bottom is used to justify disrespectful and abusive tactics. This is dangerous not only for the patients but also for the providers who wield this power. Frequently, power goes to their heads. At least half a dozen treatment programs turned into destructive cults when they applied harsh methods, starting with Synanon and imitated in Phoenix House and Daytop. For decades, such programs used sleep and food deprivation, isolation, sexual humiliation, and other abusive tactics in an attempt to get addicts to "hit bottom" and "surrender." Incredibly, many programs—particularly those that receive large numbers of patients from the criminal justice system—still use demeaning approaches.

Eventually a "tough love" approach became popular, spurred by a bestselling 1982 book by that title and a related support group, which had thousands of members during the 1980s and '90s. Members exhorted parents and spouses to stop "enabling" the addictions of their loved ones in order to help them recognize their powerlessness. Members also urged fellow parents not to bail out their kids if they were arrested. They also advised them to cut off all contact with children who were not compliant. Advocating publicly for tougher laws and for harsh, Synanon-based treatment programs like Straight, Incorporated, "tough love" supporters promoted policies that traumatized thousands of families nationally. Unfortunately, "tough love" tactics were untested before being accepted and implemented.

A widely publicized case of "tough love" involved Terry McGovern, daughter of former presidential candidate and Minnesota senator George McGovern. A counselor told the McGoverns to refuse contact with their depressed and alcoholic daughter if she kept drinking. Shortly thereafter, the McGoverns were devastated to learn that Terry had been found dead from exposure in a snowbank. Though there are clearly times when parents and loved ones need to distance themselves from addicted children for their own sanity or to protect others, there is no way to predict whether this will harm or help addicted individuals.

While the Twelve Step idea of powerlessness, improperly applied, can be harmful, it can also be counterproductive. Research shows that the more people believe in the idea that addiction is a disease over which they are powerless, the worse and more frequent their relapses tend to be. While some individuals interpret "powerlessness" spiritually, others take it literally to mean they lack control not only over drugs but also over all meaningful spheres in their lives. This can be particularly damaging to women, members of minority groups, and people with depression, inferiority, and loss of incentive.

Teaching women, youth, and other vulnerable minorities to rely on Twelve Step programs may expose them to sexual predators and to people with other antisocial personality disorders. If A.A. represents the general population of addicted people, around one in five members has a personality disorder that is marked by manipulative and dishonest behavior. Because sex offenders are often court mandated to attend Twelve Step programs, up to half of all women who join such groups experience behavior often euphemized as the "13th step," in which males try to coerce or seduce women who are new to the program. Youth, too, can be targeted in such environments, marijuana smokers and binge drinkers exposed to more potent drugs.

Twelve Step programs and the medical system should remain separate. Designed as mutual help organizations, not professional therapy, A.A. groups were never intended as medical treatment. As faith-based groups in general, Twelve Step programs are lay groups where afflicted people support one another and find God. Consequently, indoctrination into Twelve Step ideology should not be mandated by courts or be part of professional care, particularly for women, minorities, and youth. This is not to say that social and spiritual support is not valuable, but that it should be freely chosen. Such an approach reflects A.A.'s Tradition Eight, which affirms that A.A. should remain nonprofessional and that people should not be compensated for Twelve Step work. Judges, law enforcement officials, and therapists can certainly recommend Twelve Step programs, but they should never require them as official rehab. Secular alternatives like SMART Recovery and Moderation Management are available. In addition, effective therapies such as motivational enhancement therapy, MAT (medication assisted treatment), and cognitive behavioral therapy, which require trained therapists and doctors, may be necessary.

## The Potential Misuse of Power by Legal Authorities

Without doubt, the unique way America treats addicts—as morally sick and criminally guilty—reinforces stigma. Moreover, in applying this mindset, Americans are biased. Research shows that 25 percent believe discrimination against people with mental illnesses is acceptable, compared to two thirds of Americans who support employment discrimination against people with addictions. As we have noted, great harm can be inflicted when medical and criminal justice systems are combined forcibly with Twelve-Step spirituality, such as when concepts like "hitting bottom" are combined with punitive methods of treatment or with criminalization of drug use—responses ineffective and potentially harmful.

Nevertheless, conventional wisdom maintains that the more punitively addicts are treated, the more likely their recovery. Conversely, the more kindness and support they receive, the less likely they will be to stop drinking and using other drugs. While drug courts typically offer reduced sentences for complying with treatment ordered by a judge, in the past many drug court advocates argued for harsher sentences, in part because they believed addicts would not seek help unless their "bottom" was as bad as possible. Even though these assumptions are not supported by evidence, they have been used to justify punishment, cruelty, and abuse of people with addictions. Thankfully, that mindset is changing, as judges and others in authority are looking for less punitive solutions, particularly to drug possession and abuse.

As studies show, incarceration does not stop addiction. One survey of drug users in Baltimore, taken between 1988 and 2000, found that people incarcerated during that period were half as likely as those who were not to quit taking drugs. A Canadian study from 1996 through 2005 showed more dramatic results, that incarceration cut the odds of recovery by nearly half. The data on adolescents show even stronger evidence of harm. A study of one hundred thousand American adolescents arrested between 1990 and 2005—mainly for drug crimes or assault—found that those who received custodial sentences were three times more likely to be incarcerated as adults, regardless of the severity of the initial crime, as compared to those given alternative sentences in the community or those who had charges dropped. This means that for youth, prison is essentially three times worse than doing nothing at all. A Canadian study, which followed nearly eight hundred low-income youth, showed an even greater effect. It found that the adult arrest rates for people who had any previous contact with the juvenile justice system were seven times higher than those engaged in a similar level of delinquency who were not caught. Moreover, the odds of adult crime were over thirty-seven times higher if the teen had been sent to reform school or juvenile prison.[9]

When we evaluate the effectiveness of incarceration by international comparisons, the results are equally stunning. While some studies indicate no correlation between the toughness of a country's drug policy and the rates of drug use, other studies indicate that countries with the toughest drug policies often have the worst addiction problems. No country illustrates this better than the United States. According to a 2013 study, the

9. Ibid., 176–77.

United States, which leads the world in incarceration rates, also topped the charts in marijuana and cocaine addiction, suggesting that the criminal justice system is not an effective way to reduce drug-related harm. In addition, while the United States leads the world in painkiller misuse, the countries with the worst rates of heroin and opium addiction are not free societies in the West but rather hardline countries like Russia, Afghanistan, and Iran, some of which apply the death penalty for drug offenses.

When we compare drug-war spending and incarceration rates with addiction rates, the data are even more transparent. In the United States, funding for the war against drugs went from $100 million in 1970 to more than $15 billion annually in 2010, increasing by a factor of over thirty, even after accounting for inflation. During that same period, however, addiction rates remained flat or rose. In fact, between 2001 and 2005, the incarceration rates in the United States more than quadrupled, much of this increase driven by drug arrests and drug related crime. During this period, America's trillion-dollar law enforcement spending spree did not decrease addiction rates; it may actually have increased them.[10]

In light of such dismal statistics, why do many people in authority, including some running rehabs, argue that retaining criminal penalties for drug use is the only way to avoid drug epidemics? Why do many contend that treatment cannot work unless it is backed by punishment, when we know punishment does not work? Furthermore, how can advocates claim that addiction is a disease—and then argue that criminal sanction be part of the treatment—when they do not apply this to other diseases? The answers, unfortunately, have more to do with the ongoing racist and moral framing of addiction in drug policy than with the effectiveness of punishment and incarceration. Such attitudes are linked to the still prevalent misconception that locking people up during withdrawal will solve the problem, even though detox alone rarely leads to recovery.

In addition, the system is biased in favor of the majority population. While wealthy parents and people of privilege can afford to hire lawyers to protect their children from sentencing extremes, poor and racially marginalized individuals remain vulnerable. These days, the lifetime odds of going to prison for a black male in America are one in three—a figure that has doubled since Richard Nixon declared war on drugs in the 1970s. This rate is more than five times higher than for white males. The racial inequities are clearly driven by drug enforcement. A 2003 analysis found that black

10. Ibid., 178–79.

people are ten times more likely to get arrested for drug crimes, compared to whites. Conviction rates are also higher. In federal prison, on average blacks serve nearly as long for drug offenses as whites do for violent ones.[11]

While the criminal justice system may occasionally be required to fight addictive behavior, particularly when crimes are committed, the data on humiliation, isolation, punishment, and confrontation as treatment for addiction shows that punitive responses are not helpful, and furthermore, that they can lead to relapse and worsening addiction. After more than four decades of research, not a single study supports the confrontational approach as superior to kinder and less potentially harmful treatments.

A better approach exists, based on an integrative model of addiction and recovery. Because addictions represent complex interactions between biological, psychological, social, and spiritual forces, the solution must be holistic as well. The more we understand how addictive enslavement occurs, the better we may be able to turn in the direction of kindness, forgiveness, and service, as the next chapter demonstrates.

## Questions for Discussion and Reflection

1. In your own words, explain the biblical concept of "powers and principalities." Why does the Bible portray these entities as "false gods"?

2. How can followers of Christ defeat "false powers"?

3. Explain and assess the merits of Anne Schaef's claim that "human society shows all the signs of classic addiction."

4. Evaluate Jefferson Singer's critique of the Twelve Step approach to recovery. While the A.A. narrative is compelling, what are its limitations?

5. What dangers lurk when Twelve Step morality is highjacked by coercive criminal justice systems or by secular hospital-based treatment centers?

6. Explain why punishment or incarceration are ineffective over drug possession or addictive drug use.

11. Ibid., 226–27.

7. According to this chapter, what is the "problem with bottom"? Do you agree or disagree with the concept of "hitting bottom" in recovery? Explain your answer.

8. Evaluate the merits of the "tough love" approach by families of addicted individuals.

9. In your estimation, what is the primary insight gained from this chapter?

10. *For personal reflection*: Does this chapter raise any issues you might need to address in the future?

CHAPTER 10

# Awareness and Love

God is love. And those who abide in love abide in God,
and God abides in them . . . We love, because [God] first loved us.
—1 JOHN 4:16, 19.

IN THE BEGINNING WAS . . . Love! Love is the act of will that at the beginning
of time brought forth life. Love—God, energy, Being—is the primal force
in the universe. Without love, nothing can exist. With love, all is possible.

## Original Love: The "Pattern of Creation"

In the second account of creation (found in Genesis 2–3. the so-called
"J account of creation"), the author focuses on two sets of relationships:
theological (issues related to the vertical relationship between humans and
God) and sociological (issues related to the horizontal relationship, that
between humans). The primary thrust of the story is vertical, having to do
with the rule of God and the nature of human destiny. Both agendas belong
together. The first story, the "pattern of creation" (described in Genesis
2:1–25 and central to the theological agenda) represents harmony between
humans and God, nature, others, and self. To illustrate, envision a large
circle with four compass points (north representing God, south representing Nature, east representing Others, and west representing Self). Within
that circle, imagine a smaller circle, representing the individual ego or self;

then four lines emanating from the smaller circle toward the four compass points, each line an arrow pointing outward.

The second story, the "pattern of the fall," (described in Genesis 3:1–24 and central to the sociological agenda), shows the distortion of human community that comes from human autonomy, that is, human rebellion against the pattern of creation. The result is disharmony with God, nature, others, and self. Disobedience (the "pattern of the fall") represents a reversal of the pattern of creation, the four arrows or lines in our illustration now pointing inward. The illustration of the biblical "fall from grace" helps us better understand addiction, what the Bible calls sin. Addiction is sin because it reflects the pattern of the fall, the self incurably turned inward. Addictions are obsessions gone viral. They occur when something natural and good (self-love, pleasure, happiness) goes bad. The Bible describes the threefold nature of the human spiritual condition thus: God creates us for love and freedom, attachment hinders us, and grace is necessary for our salvation (the transformation necessary for our release from attachment and bondage to addiction).

## The God-Shaped Vacuum in Every Human Heart

The famous French mathematician and philosopher Blaise Pascal spoke inspirationally when he declared: "There is a God-shaped vacuum in the heart of each person that cannot be satisfied by any created thing but only by God the Creator, made known through Jesus Christ." Psychiatrist Gerald May agrees with Pascal when he writes, "I am convinced that all human beings have an inborn desire for God. Whether we are consciously religious or not, this desire is our deepest longing and our most precious treasure . . . Some of us have repressed this desire, burying it beneath so many other interests that we are completely unaware of it. Or we may experience it in different ways—as a longing for wholeness, completion, or fulfillment. Regardless of how we describe it, it is a longing for love. It is a hunger to love, to be loved, and to move closer to the Source of love. This yearning is the essence of the human spirit, the origin of our highest hopes and most noble dreams."[1]

From a psychoanalytic perspective, we might say that humans displace their longing for God upon other things. Behaviorally, humans are conditioned to seek objects by the positive and negative reinforcements of

1. May, *Addiction and Love*, 1.

their own private experience and by the messages of parents, peers, and culture. Even the briefest look at television, magazine, and Internet advertising reveals how strongly culture reinforces attachment to things other than God, and what high value it places on willful self-determination and mastery. Mediating the stimuli they receive, the cells of our brains continually seek equilibrium, developing patterns of adaptation that constitute what is normal. Thus, the more we become accustomed to seeking spiritual satisfaction through things other than God, the more abnormal and stressful it becomes to look for God directly.

When we first reclaim our spiritual longing, we usually do not know that the journey homeward involves relinquishment of self, that the process is so painful and difficult. The greater danger, however, is that those who think they understand the process are likely to try to make it happen on their own, by engaging in false austerities and love-denying deprivations. They will not wait for God's timing; they will rush ahead of grace. This can happen in two ways, when people overinstitutionalize the journey, that is, when people become addicted to religious methods or institutions, or when individuals think they can engineer their own redemption. However, if we allow grace to guide our response, we will realize what we need to know as we need to know it.

In letting go of addictions, one of the most frightening realizations is that there is no new normality of freedom to replace the old patterns. This lack of normality is actually caused by God, for there can be no addiction to the true God, since God refuses to be an object. While God, perhaps best characterized as "the flow between things,"[2] is ever-present, the one passionate and faithful Lover of our lives, God is never ordinary or "normal," and rarely present, as things are present. If lack of normality is true of God, massive implications follow for the conduct of the spiritual life. We all want clear steps to follow, prescribed methods of living and knowing God and staying on track spiritually, but that kind of security and guidance does not exist. Addiction to religious systems, like addiction to anything else, brings slavery, not freedom. The structures of religion are meant to mediate God's self-revelation through community; they are not meant to be substitute gods. Doctrines of belief, moral standards, and reliance on scripture are all essential aspects of authentic spirituality. Sacraments, too, are special

---

2. This understanding guides Richard Rohr's definition of God in his 2016 book, *The Divine Dance.*

means of grace. All are vehicles for God's love, but addiction to them makes them obstacles to the freedom required for growth and transformed lives.

We can temporarily make images of God, freedom, love, and grace, and try to form them into new normalities to which we can cling, but these attachments must eventually be lifted as well. Authentic freedom and love cannot be captured by attachment. Therefore, the journey home does not lead toward new, more sophisticated addictions, or even toward new self-images, for they too can become addictive. While the process of re-linquishment—biologically speaking—is really only a matter of easing the power that certain cell systems have over our sense of self—it can feel like death. And it is, spiritually speaking, because without death there can be no resurrection, no lasting transformation. If the journey is truly homeward, it leads toward liberation from addiction altogether. Obviously, this is a lifelong process.

There is a pathetic grandeur in the picture of Adam reaching to taste the fruit of the tree of knowledge of good and evil. Knowledge is human-kind's capacity. Freedom to leave the innocence of childhood is precisely what elevates humans above the animals. But when humanity's capacity for knowledge becomes the occasion for arrogant power and self-exaltation, inevitably it results in a fall from the life of trust and goodness that God intends. We cannot recover the mythological innocence of Adam, nor can we return to a Garden that is a figment of the religious imagination. Never-theless, through revelation humans know there is a better way, the way life can and should be.

While the pattern of the fall ends with the expulsion of Adam and Eve from the Garden, there is good news here. Graciousness appears in the nar-rative in 3:21, where God clothes the hapless couple, mercifully shielding them from their shame and giving them a new start, for they get to live and try anew. The ending is hopeful for it represents a new beginning.

## The Four Loves[3]

We have used the word "love" repeatedly in our study, but it is time we clarify what we mean by love, for the word is easily misunderstood in the English language. In his classic book, *The Four Loves*, C. S. Lewis examines four words found in the Greek language to describe four basic kinds of love:

3. The material in this segment is adapted from my *Living Graciously on Planet Earth*, 97–101.

1. *Love as Affection* (*storgē*): this love refers to familial bonds of love;

2. *Love as Friendship* (*philia*): here love refers to companionship, to love between friends;

3. *Love as Romance* (*eros*): this love refers primarily to the erotic or sexual bonds of love;

4. *Love as Commitment* (*agapē*): here we are speaking of love that is supernatural, spiritual, and unconditional; charitable love.

It is the last of these to which Paul refers in 1 Corinthians 13, using a term traditionally translated as "charity." That translation is misunderstood in today's culture, for it has come to be associated mostly with administering relief to people in need, and that is not what Paul had in mind. Agape is more than generosity and clearly transcends human affection.

Of the four terms for love, the first three generally refer to "love of the deserving," and this is not the meaning Paul wishes to convey. What makes agape unique is that it alone clearly means "love of the undeserving." The classic expression of agape love is Romans 5:8: "But God shows his love for us in that while we were yet sinners Christ died for us." Such love, clearly "love of the undeserving," is rooted in grace.

Can such love be described? Paul attempts to do so in 1 Corinthians 13, saying that "love is patient; love is kind; love is not envious or boastful or arrogant or rude. Love does not insist on its own way; it is not irritable or resentful; it does not rejoice in wrongdoing, but rejoices in the truth. Love bears all things, believes all things, hopes all things, endures all things." If I do not have love, says Paul, "I am nothing"; whatever my privilege, service, or even virtue, if I do not have love, "I gain nothing."

If agape is a divine quality, can humans participate in such love? To that question the scriptures answer with a resounding "Yes!" But we must begin, not with mysticism—with the creature's love for God—but at the start of all things, with Love as the divine energy. In God there is no hunger that needs to be filled, only plenteousness that desires to give: "God so loved the world that he gave his only Son" (John 3:16). This is a depiction of God as Lover, the inventor of all loves. C. S. Lewis calls this primal love "Gift-love."

According to Lewis, God, as creator, implants in humans both "Gift-loves" and "Need-loves."[4] Gift-loves are exhibited naturally, such as in

4. Lewis, *Four Loves*, 176.

the love of a devoted mother or of a benevolent ruler. In addition to these natural gifts, God bestows "Divine Gift-love," working directly in us. Such love enables us to love lavishly or selflessly, including those who are not naturally loveable (lepers, criminals, enemies). God's Gift-love also enables humans to have

Need-love toward God. Thus, God's Gift-love bestows on humans a double Need-love:

- supernatural Need-love of God and

- supernatural Need-love of one another.

Remarkably, God turns our need of God into Need-love of God, and stranger still, creates in us an unnatural receptivity of love from our fellow humans. This includes their love for the unlovable in us. Thus God, admitted to the human heart, transforms not only Gift-love but Need-love; not only our Need-love of God, but our Need-love of one another. And that is the task of true spirituality, the invitation to turn our natural loves into agape love, or more specifically, to let God turn our love into agape. Such a task requires renewal of our hearts and minds, a radical change called conversion, which transforms us from "getting" people to "giving" people. This transformation is beyond human possibility. The Christian message is that humans can only experience this makeover when Christ is "formed" in them (Gal. 4:19).

For Lewis, human agape love is not an emotional state but a volitional one, not a state of the feelings but of the will, what we might call "possibility thinking." Agape love is not about liking someone or even about fondness, but rather about "acting as if." In the Bible, one loves God by loving others. And the starting point is to "behave as if" we loved others, because to do so leads to agape. As soon as we engage in such possibility thinking we discover one of life's great truths, that when we behave as if we love someone, we come to love them. The reverse is also true: if we ill-treat others, we come to hate and despise them. And the more cruel we are, the more we will hate—others and God. The key point to remember is that though our feelings for God and others come and go, God's love for us does not.

The foundational principle of Christian spirituality is that our spiritual health is in proportion to our love for God. Ironically, humans approach God most nearly when they are in one sense least like God. For what can be more unlike than fullness and need, sovereignty and humility, righteousness and penitence, limitless power and helplessness? In our love of God, we begin practically, with deeds of kindness, with forgiveness, remembering that good, like evil, increases exponentially. That is why the small decisions we make are of such importance. Writing during World War II, Lewis states: "The smallest good act today is the capture of a strategic point from which, a few months later, you may be able to go on to victories you never dreamed of. An apparently trivial indulgence in lust or anger today is the loss of a ridge or railway line or bridgehead from which the enemy may launch an attack otherwise impossible."[5]

As Lewis reminds us, God, who needs nothing, loves into existence superfluous creatures in order to perfect them. It is easy to acknowledge, but almost impossible to realize for long, that we are mirrors whose brightness, if we are bright, is wholly derived from the sun that shines upon us. God is love, and we can all slowly develop in agape love as we begin to grow in Christ, illumined by natural and supernatural grace.

According to Paul, agape is superior to all virtues, including the supernatural ones: "now faith, hope, and love abide, these three; and the greatest of these is love." Without agape, all spiritual gifts are empty and vain. Earnestly desire the spiritual gifts, we are told in 1 Corinthians 14:1, but make agape your aim.

Agape is superior, says Paul, because love "never ends," meaning literally "love never collapses" (1 Cor. 13:8). Love never fails because it is an extension of God's eternal nature (1 John 4:8). Furthermore, love is superior because while faith and hope are designated for the present life, agape is the way of life in the new creation we await. So to love with agape love now is to live proleptically, out of the resources of the future, and when people live that way, they demonstrate not only the reality of eternal life but also the fact that it is available in the present and not merely as a future hope.

Agape, as an attitude of the heart, mind, and will, energizes and activates the whole of one's personality. Agape love is the highest form of knowing, the highest form of being, and the highest form of living. Such love is only possible for those who live in the power of the indwelling Spirit.

We know the story of Mother Teresa, how she devoted her life to serving untouchables in Calcutta. A reporter once asked her the secret of her remarkable ministry, wondering how she accomplished such acts of love. Mother Teresa responded by pointing upward and then saying: "He has done it all. I have done nothing." On another occasion she pointed out that human holiness (namely, our role in God's work of love) does not consist in

5. Lewis, *Mere Christianity*, 117.

doing *extraordinary* deeds but rather in doing *ordinary* deeds passionately, with great love.

Faith, hope, and love, these three principles, taken together, are guaranteed to transform our lives. We start with faith, with unconditional trust in God and in God's faithfulness. Faith leads to hope, joyful confidence in the future because God is in charge, and out of that hope comes agape, unconditional "love of the undeserving," manifested fully in Jesus Christ and in all who follow in his steps, including saints like Mother Teresa and like you and me, unworthy yet saved (transformed) by grace.

According to scripture, love is not something humans produce or earn. Love is a gift of grace, built into the cosmos by a loving Presence. Loving may be displayed in acts of kindness, but it is not primarily about others. Love is primarily about one's relationship with God. Those who love the cosmos, including all its creatures and manifestations, are said to be like God, happy and fulfilled. In the New Testament, love is the law of the new order. God's people are to show love unconditionally, without expecting it to be returned. The basis for such love is God's love, evidence in Jesus, God's gift of love for the world. Love may have four meanings, but it is agape, meaning "love of the undeserving," that we envision when we speak of love as a virtue.

## The Power of Love

As an alcoholic friend described it, addiction affects heart and spirit as well as mind and body. The symptoms of addiction are physical compulsion, mental obsession, emotional duress, and spiritual deficiency. Driven by distorted living and thinking, the addict is beyond help. Where does one go from here? The answer is found in the second step of the Twelve Step approach: "*came to believe that a Power greater than ourselves could restore us to sanity,*" and Step Three: "*made a decision to turn our will and our lives over to the care of God as we understood Him.*" For many, practicing these steps causes a chain reaction that can be described as atomic, in that it releases a power—a divine energy—present all along but only now apprehended and utilized. Enacting these steps connects us with real love, and we know what real love does: it changes outcomes and transforms people. Divine power, coupled with human powerlessness, produces a spiritual chemical reaction that is transformative, the gift of unconditional grace. The truth underlying Step Three is clear: "When you and God agree on something, nothing is impossible" (see Gen. 18:14; Jer. 32:17). As the apostle Paul affirmed, "If God is for us, who is against us?" (Rom. 8:31).

## Holistic Therapy

The biopsychosocial model, a modern holistic view of human beings now increasingly used in health sciences, was introduced to medicine by George L. Engel (1913–1999), a prominent scholar engaged in the psychosomatic movement. He claimed that in order to better understand and respond to patients' needs, physicians should simultaneously attend to the biological, psychological, and social dimensions of an illness. This approach views suffering, disease, and illness as affected by multiple factors, from societal to molecular. At a practical level, it is a way of understanding the patient's subjective experience as an essential contributor not only to human care and accurate diagnosis, but also to health outcome.[6]

In recent decades, humanization of medicine and empowerment of patients have been improved by including the patient's subjective experience, by expanding the causational framework of disease, by valuating the patient-clinician relationship, and by giving expanding roles to the patient in clinical decision-making. In 1948, the World Health Organization (WHO) adopted the following definition of health: "Health is a state of complete physical, mental, and social well-being, and not merely the absence of disease or infirmity." This definition, while expansive, lacked reference to the spiritual dimension of life. However, in 1999, the 52nd Assembly of this institution proposed some amendments to its constitution. One of the proposed modifications was the insertion of spiritual well-being into its concept of health. The new text became, "Health is a dynamic state of complete physical, mental, spiritual, and social well-being and not merely the absence of disease or infirmity." Despite approval, the new version was eventually rejected, partly because of the ambiguous nature and the multiple meanings of the concept of spirituality, though the WHO continues to highlight the importance of the spiritual dimension for clinical purposes.

Currently, many researchers are expanding the biopsychosocial model to include the spiritual dimension. One such researcher is David A. Katerndahl, whose study "Impact of Spiritual Symptoms and Their Interactions on Health Services and Life Satisfaction" demonstrates the relevance

---

6. Saad, "A True Biopsychosocial-Spiritual Model?"

of spirituality for understanding health outcomes.[7] Likewise, Daniel P. Sulmasy justifies the expansion of the model to psychosocial-spiritual by noting that genuinely holistic health care must address the totality of the patient's relational existence. According to Sulmasy, this expansion will contribute to a model of care and research that takes account of patients in their entirety.[8]

Psychologists are now referring to this integrative model of addiction and recovery as the Bio-Psycho-Social-Spiritual Model (BPSS). This approach maintains that all addictions represent a complex interaction between biological, psychological, social, and spiritual forces. From the BPSS perspective, addiction is a complex and dynamic process. This model is not as simple as the disease model, where one either has an addiction (a disease) or not. According to the BPSS model, addiction problems may range in severity from none to severe, and this can change across a person's life.

Using alcohol as an example, the spectrum would include abstainers, low risk or "social" drinkers (moderate risk), medium risk drinkers, and high-risk drinkers. This scale can also be characterized as the no use-use-abuse-addiction continuum. Because the BPSS model addresses a broad range of problems, from none to severe, the model also implies different recovery approaches, varying according to the severity of a person's problem. For some people, moderation might be best, while for others complete abstinence may be required. Because the BPSS model allows for greater complexity than the disease concept of addiction, and because it takes into consideration the spiritual dimension of life, it more holistically captures the causes and the solutions to the problem of addiction.

## Love and Service

In his final message to his friends in recovery, Dr. Bob (cofounder of A.A.) summarized the Twelve Step program in three phrases—Trust God, Clean House, and Help Others—and in two words—Love and Service. These two concepts, it turns out, summarize Jesus' message regarding human obligation: "you shall love the Lord your God with all your heart, and with all your soul, and with all your strength, and with all your mind; and your neighbor as yourself" (Luke 10:27). Service involves two interrelated dimensions: love of God, manifested in worship, and love of neighbor, manifested in

7. Katerndahl, "Impact of Spiritual Symptoms," 412–20.
8. Sulmasy, "Biopsychosocial-Spiritual Model," 24–33.

bringing joy to others and in addressing human need. To worship is to experience God, and to experience God is to love and serve others. In the words of Brian McLaren, "There is nothing more radically activist than a truly spiritual life, and there is nothing more truly spiritual than a radically activist life."[9] Victory over addiction, while virtually impossible without outside assistance, becomes practically effortless with divine help.

As people in recovery know, letting go of addiction is not possible without the transformative power of love. By love, I do not mean sentimentality, although human emotion is certainly involved, but unconditional love. The source of such love in the universe, the author of unconditional love, is God. For that reason, when the Bible defines God, it states that God is love (1 John 4:16). Unconditional love (agape), while it cannot be manufactured or produced by mortal creatures, can be displayed by human beings. Such love requires the orientation of one's life toward a center outside of oneself, a recognition that one's value is not absolute but derives from relationship to God. Love can only be acquired in the confidence that it has already been given." As we read in the First Epistle of John: "We love, because he first loved us" (1 John 4:19). When we know we are forgiven and loved unconditionally, we come to value other people and things as they are related to God and not as they are useful or important to ourselves. This understanding of love, as divine gift, consistently functions in ways that enable others to flourish with their own dignity and their own relationship to God.

Service is an important tool for remaining free of addictive patterns and behavior. In addition to volunteering locally, such as in food banks, Special Olympics, Cancer Society and American Lung association programs, helping in nursing homes, visiting the elderly, or participating in other ministries to people in need, there are many options available for doing service through Twelve Step programs in your community. These include becoming a sponsor, volunteering to help with an existing meeting, organizing social events, making phone calls, answering mail, and leading workshops or book studies.

Because of God, the universe is a love dispensing entity. While ordinary relationships and even sexuality can take place without love, human addiction cannot be defeated without divine love, that is, without God. On their own, out of their own resources, humans may be able to eliminate one or more addictions, but the net result is the substitution of one addiction by

9. McLaren, *Naked Spirituality*, 237.

another, more virulent type, one form of self-sufficiency and self-control by another. As Einstein noted, "no problem can be solved from the same level of consciousness that created it."

## Questions for Discussion and Reflection

1. Do you agree with the statement that love is the primal force in the universe? Explain your answer.

2. With respect to Genesis 2–3, explain the difference between the biblical "pattern of creation" and the "pattern of the fall." What do these contrasting perspectives reveal about the nature of addiction?

3. What did Pascal mean by the "God-shaped vacuum" within each person? Do you agree with his view? Explain your answer.

4. In your estimation, what is the difference between addiction to religion and a relationship with the true God? Explain and assess the merits of the view that "there can be no addiction to the true God."

5. Describe your understanding of the Greek word agape. Are there people in your life you love in this manner? Are there people in your life you need to love in this manner? Why or why not?

6. What is the difference between "Gift-love" and "Need-love"? In your own words, explain the meaning of the statement, "God's Gift-love enables humans to have Need-love for one another."

7. Describe the four areas of life affected by one's addiction, and how these four dimensions can be transformed by the power of divine love.

8. In your estimation, what is the primary insight gained from this chapter?

9. *For personal reflection*: How has divine help contributed to your victory over addiction?

10. *For personal reflection*: Does this chapter raise any issues you might need to address in the future?

CHAPTER 11

# Awareness and Grace

No problem can be solved from the same level of consciousness that created it.

—ALBERT EINSTEIN

WE ALL ORIGINATE IN freedom, and we are meant for freedom. Addiction, however, holds us back from our rightful destiny; it makes us prisoners of our own impulses and slaves to our own selfish idols. This is our condition, something the scriptures of all the world's religions attest.

According to the Bible, God creates each person uniquely, and, as the psalmist affirms, our creation is good: "For it was you who formed my inward parts; you knit me together in my mother's womb. I praise you, for I am fearfully and wonderfully made" (Ps. 139:13–14). God's intention, the prophet Jeremiah attests, affects not only our potential at birth but also our life's journey. God lovingly creates us for a lifetime of fullness and freedom: "I know the plans I have for you, says the Lord, plans for your welfare and not for harm, to give you a future with hope" (Jer. 29:11). Finally, God creates us for love; the call of our creation is for us to love God, one another, and ourselves: "You shall love the Lord your God with all your heart, and with all your soul, and with all your mind, and with all your strength . . . and your neighbor as yourself" (Mark 12:30–31). Our ultimate allegiance, of course, is to God: "you shall have no other gods" (Exod. 20: 3). The biblical explanation is clear: There is within ever human being an innate yearning for God, and this yearning is our most precious treasure, for it gives human existence meaning and direction.

Nevertheless, as the account of the Garden in Genesis indicates, our creation also includes temptation and attachment. Because God appears remote and inaccessible, and material objects and pleasurable experiences appear visible, available, and ubiquitous, we attempt to fulfill our longing for God through attachment. For example, God wants to be our perfect lover, but instead we seek perfection in human relationships and are disappointed when our lovers cannot love us perfectly. God wants to provide our ultimate security, but we seek safety in power and possessions and then find we must worry about them continually. We seek satisfaction of our spiritual longing in a host of ways that may have very little to do with God, and, eventually, we become disappointed. Because of this, our love of God, neighbor, and self is tainted, and we are not fully free to follow God's call with our own power. We must struggle, and we stand in need of grace. The solution—detachment—is simple. Like falling asleep, the transfer of power is natural and effortless—hence it is called "grace." Implementing grace, however—letting go—can be impossible, like trying to fall asleep when your mind is active or stressed.

Grace is as easy—and as difficult—as falling asleep. If we struggle or resist, it doesn't produce results. To let go of addictions, we may need additional help. In that case, grace may come in the form of external help, such as from a spiritual advisor, a Gestalt therapist or pastoral care minister, or free online assistance, such as Richard Rohr's daily meditations. You may also wish to learn more about your personality type (see the discussion in chapter 12). However, without relinquishment, there can be no spiritual growth.

## Grace at Work in Individuals

In *The Covenant*, a novel on South Africa, James Michener introduces a stimulating concept: "Often in the biographies of important women and men," he writes, "one comes across the phrase, 'Like a burst of light, the idea which would animate her life came upon her.'" When the Scriptures exhort us to love the Lord with all our heart, soul, mind, and strength, and our neighbor as ourselves, we come across such a concept, namely, that we are not being asked to try harder or to dig deeper into our own resources. Rather, divine resources always accompany God's commands. The supernatural virtues, available to help us live graciously, are powered by two transformative principles: (a) God never asks of us something we cannot do, and (b) when God is in agreement with us on something, nothing can stop us in our purpose.

Paul knew the meaning of those principles, practicing them regularly. As he indicated in Philippians, a letter written from prison: "I can do all things through [Christ] who strengthens me" (Phil. 4:13). Despite his circumstances, incarcerated falsely and illegally, Paul experienced the grace of God to be active and effective. When utilized, he writes elsewhere, this power can accomplish most anything: "My grace is sufficient for you, for power is made perfect in weakness" (2 Cor. 12:9).

Before there was a universe, even before love, there was grace. Grace, like faith, hope, and love, cannot simply be learned through practice, as other human virtues are. Either we have grace as a gift, or our efforts to change habits and behavior are doomed to failure. Grace, the foundation upon which all liberation rests, is life's most transformative concept. The starting point for victory over addiction is this: We live in a gracious universe, created by Love and perpetuated by Spirit. And this grace is available—already embraces—all creatures, indeed, all life.

Aligned with the tradition that affirms God as creator of the world, we affirm that in God's provision for the beings that issue from God's creativity, grace is built into the processes of birth, of maternal or parental care, and into the orders that humans have developed for the sustenance and maintenance of life. To this grace, which we might call "ordinary grace," we add "extraordinary grace," which brings the unpredictable and unexpected manifestation of divine transformative power to our lives and accompanies God's work of righteousness and liberation in our world.

Christian grace offers a relationship between God and morality quite different from the one often imagined. In Christ, God meets us not only as lawgiver and judge but primarily as the One who graciously accepts us despite our failure to live up to what God requires, and who restores our hope for the future despite our inability to make up for what society failed to do in the past. We encounter this gracious God both at the beginning of our thinking about addiction and even more precisely in the pain and confusion of actual addictive behavior. If we accept the grace God offers, we are freed from the weight of our past and our hope is restored. If we refuse grace, our moral life is apt to become a deceptive exercise in justifying our mistakes and blaming our failures on others. On the other hand, we may slide into the despair of moral failure, unable to undo the wrong we have done and hopeless about our future. Only a gracious God keeps our moral life from becoming a constant measurement of ourselves against a standard we can never meet, anticipating a dreadful judgment we can never escape.

This does not mean that there is no law or judgment in Christian ethics. People have misunderstood God's grace in that way ever since some told Paul that their response to the gospel would be to continue in sin so that grace may abound (Rom. 6:1). Christian ethics does mean, however, that the moral life is not one long preparation for judgment that lies ahead. The Christian truth is that judgment has already happened, in the death and resurrection of Jesus Christ. And because judgment is covered by grace, we are free to reorient our moral lives toward the future rather than continually reviewing the failures of the past.

When we encounter a gracious God in the midst of life, we can live faithfully, hopefully, and lovingly, perhaps for the very first time. We need no longer live according to someone else's pattern, but we can find the goals and virtues that allow us to live a good life in our own situation, with the abilities and limitations that we actually have. We are free to build relationships and share commitments with others, living by the virtues that make a good life possibly, as we understand them, and not by someone else's rules. So the moral life, instead of being a way to defend ourselves, becomes a way to love our neighbors and God as well.

All paths to recovery and transformation embody grace, an ingredient indispensable to growth and change. If grace can be said to underlie the Christian gospel and to embody the biblical portrayal of God's identity and activity, what does the word "grace" mean, and what is its power? For the purpose of this study, I would like to define grace as "the transformative power of God at work in overcoming harmful addictions and temptations in our life."

The following biblical principles set the stage for our thinking about grace:[1]

1.  God's grace is *abundant*. As God gave "great power" and "great grace" to the early apostles (Acts 4:33), God can do the same for us, since God shows no partiality (Acts 10:34; Rom. 2:11).

---

1. The material in this segment is abridged from the discussion in *Grace Revealed*, my commentary on Paul's letter to the Romans, 37–41.

2. God's grace is *free*. In the New Testament, the words for "gift" and "grace" are closely related. This connection is made clear in passages such as Ephesians 4:7: "each of us was given *grace* according to the measure of Christ's *gift*" and 1 Corinthians 1:4–8, where the *grace* of God is said to enrich believers in all speech and knowledge, so that they are not lacking in any spiritual *gift*. The New Testament describes those who have been transformed by God's grace to be recipients of spiritual gifts (see 1 Corinthians 12–14 and Romans 12:3–21), and exhorts believers to employ their "gifts" for one another, "as stewards of the manifold grace of God" (1 Pet. 4:10).

3. God's grace is *powerful*. God exhorts us to "grow in grace" (2 Pet. 3:18), that is, to become mighty and strong in grace (2 Tim. 2:1), and this occurs when we allow God to train and nurture us. In 1 Corinthians 15:10 Paul describes grace as the enabling power of his work. Grace provides forgiveness, cleanses from all unrighteousness, and then fills us with power to press on in the "obedience of faith" (Rom. 1:5; 16:26). The wondrous truth is that this power is present not only in the work of regeneration, but at every stage of the Christian life (1 Pet. 4:10–11; 2 Thess. 1:11–12).

4. God's grace is *transformative*. The Bible teaches that we cannot reach our divine destiny by relying on our own wisdom, knowledge, intelligence, or strength, for those who try to build the house of their lives solely through their own efforts will end up laboring in vain (Ps. 127:1). However, we will reach our destiny if God guides our steps and nourishes our vision with transformative power and grace: "Not by might, nor by power, but by my spirit, says the Lord of hosts" (Zech. 4:6).

The concept of grace, lavish and free, can be easily misunderstood, and consequently abused (see Rom. 2:3–4; 3:8; 6:1–2, 15). In his Christian classic *The Cost of Discipleship*, German theologian Dietrich Bonhoeffer (1906–1945) wrote an exposition on the Sermon on the Mount in which he spells out what it means to follow Christ. First published in 1937 under the title "Discipleship," Bonhoeffer wrote when the rise of Nazism was underway in Germany, and against that backdrop developed his theology of costly discipleship, which led to his premature death in 1945. In this book, Bonhoeffer presented his audience with a profound understanding of grace by distinguishing between "cheap grace" and "costly grace."

Cheap grace, Bonhoeffer argued, is grace without discipleship or the cross, grace apart from the living and incarnate Jesus Christ. Cheap grace is a byproduct of the spread of Christianity, which resulted in secularization and in the church's accommodation to the requirements of society. Cheap grace is represented as grace without price; grace without cost.

Costly grace is the call of Jesus Christ at which disciples leave their nets and follow him. Such grace is costly because it calls us to follow, and it is grace because it calls us to follow Jesus Christ. It is costly because it costs our lives, and it is grace because it gives us the only true life. It is costly because it condemns sin, and grace because it justifies the sinner. It is costly because it compels a person to submit to the yoke of Christ and follow him, and grace because Jesus says: "My yoke is easy and my burden is light" (Matt. 11:30). Above all, it is costly because it cost God the life of the Son: "You were bought with a price" (1 Cor. 6:20), and what cost God much cannot be cheap for us. Costly grace represents the incarnation of God.

In Germany Bonhoeffer opposed Hitler's social and political agenda, and was arrested in 1943, after being associated with a plot to assassinate Adolf Hitler. After imprisonment he was sent to a concentration camp, where he was executed by hanging days before the collapse of the Nazi regime. Bonhoeffer chose costly grace over cheap grace; in death he embraced the cost of discipleship, faithful to the end.

Of all the attributes of Jesus Christ in the New Testament, perhaps the most significant is "full of grace" (John 1:12), a grace he shares lavishly with his followers, as John's Gospel makes clear: "From his fullness we have all received, grace upon grace" (John 1:16). As we learn in Ephesians 4:7, Christ delights in sharing grace with his followers.

## The Third Incarnation of God

When ordinary people become Christians, that is, "little Christ's," they embody or enact in their lives the "third incarnation" of God, or the "second coming" of Christ.[2] Let me explain what I mean. The first incarnation is the moment described in Genesis 1 as "the first day", when God became the Universal Christ, joining in unity with the physical universe and becoming the light inside of everything. This is described in Genesis 1:3–4 by the statement, "Then God said, 'Let there be light'; and there was light . . . and

2. The concept of three incarnations, exemplified in what Richard Rohr calls an incarnational worldview, is articulated in his book *The Universal Christ*, 12–21.

God separated the light from the darkness." This teaching is affirmed in the prologue of John's Gospel, by the relationship between God and Christ (the Word/Logos): "In the beginning was the Word, and the Word was with God, and the Word was God . . . in him was life, and the life was the light of all people. The light shines in the darkness, and the darkness did not overcome it" (John 1:1, 4–5). The first incarnation—what we might call the Universal Christ—is the divine presence pervading creation since the beginning. What scientists call the Big Bang is the scientific name for that event, and "Christ" is its theological name. From this perspective, wherever the material and the spiritual coincide, we have the Christ.

The second incarnation of God and the "first coming" of Christ represent what Christians believe about the historical incarnation we call Jesus. Let us be clear: Christ is not Jesus' last name. The word Christ is a title, meaning Anointed One. When Christians speak of Jesus Christ, they include the entire sweep of the meaning of the Christ, which includes all the divine activity since the beginning of time (see Romans 1:20; Hebrews 1:3; Colossians 3:11). Of this activity, Jesus is the visible map, the one who brings this eternal message home personally.

The third incarnation of God (the "second coming of Christ") occurs whenever true discipleship occurs, when Jesus Christ is born in us. This stunning possibility should not come as a shock, for we sing its truth every Christmas. Phillips Brooks spoke of this reality in the lyrics to the carol, *O Little Town of Bethlehem*:

> O holy Child of Bethlehem, Descend to us, we pray;
> Cast out our sin and enter in, *Be born in us today.*
> We hear the Christmas angels, the great glad tidings tell;
> *O come to us, abide with us, Our Lord Emmanuel.*

While Christmas captures the mystery of incarnation—of divine love and peace on earth—consumerism has turned it into a buying frenzy, beginning earlier each year, adding Black Friday and Cyber Monday to the "shop 'til we drop" mentality, all in an attempt to alleviated the anxiety of last minute shopping. How is it that a season of joy has become a season of depression and despair? Substituting consumption for spirituality always leaves us disappointed, unfulfilled, and wanting more: societal addiction at its worst!

Further evidence for the third incarnation appears in the Eucharist: "Eat it and know who you are," Augustine said. As any nutritionist knows, we are what we eat and drink. Christians are part of the Christ mystery. No longer alienated from God, others, or the universe—at least in principle—Christians embody cosmic belonging, oneness with Christ, the name we give to everything purposeful and harmonious in the universe. Paul affirmed this truth when he declared, "It is no longer I who live, but it is Christ who lives in me" (Gal. 2:20). Exhorting believers to adopt the mind of Jesus (Phil. 2:5), he also confirmed that Christians incarnate Christ, since they possess "the mind of Christ" (1 Cor. 2:16). When individuals become Jesus people—incarnations of Christ—they exchange one mindset for another, their "monkey mind" (the obsessive, noisy chattering we observe during silent meditation) for the mind of Christ.

Speaking humanistically, grace rarely means getting what we want, for God is not a permissive parent, but speaking spiritually, grace means always getting what we want, for our desires become the desires of Christ. This is likely what Paul meant when he called believers God's "new creation" (2 Cor. 5:17): "If anyone is in Christ, there is a new creation: everything old has passed away; see, everything has become new." For Paul, when the minds of believers are transformed into the mind of Christ, their bodies become temples, dwelling places of God's Spirit (1 Cor. 3:16–17; see Rom. 12:1–2).

As we travel inward, into the interior depth of soul, we discover that each believer is a chip off the old block, a miniature word of the Word of God, a mini-incarnation of divine love. This entails allowing God's grace to heal, hold, and empower us. It means entering the unknowns of our lives, and learning to trust the darkness, for the transformative power of divine love is already there.

## Grace at Work in Society

When Christians say they believe in the incarnation—that God became flesh—they are affirming a process that continues through discipleship. As the life of Jesus demonstrates, God grows with humanity, loving the earth, its creatures, and every human being through disciples, those who respond to his call to live caringly, lovingly, and faithfully. In the fourth century, when Christianity became imperial, when the cross became welded to the sword, Christianity chose a different path, based on power and theological certainty rather than on compassionate service and sacrificial love, the basis of incarnational discipleship. This resulted in Christendom, a self-serving, entitled form of Christianity addicted to power and control. Incarnational thinking is transformative when it results in incarnational living, not in imperial dominance and control.

An alternative to the war on drugs in America, known as "harm reduction," is beginning to take shape. Since the 1980s, when it originated, this approach recognized the failure of punishment or threat to solve drug addiction. Based on the idea that even during active addiction, people can learn and change, it affirms the crucial role of learning in addiction. As with all learning, however, what matters is what works best for each individual. As there are many ways to learn, there are many ways to recover. If addiction is driven by learning—not just by exposure to a particular substance, having certain genetic traits, or being traumatized—then to effectively address addiction, we need to recognize that no single treatment can possibly fit all. People have individual needs, and as they learn, they mature, resulting in different outcomes.

If the starting point for successful learning is a climate of compassion and respect, then this is how society must help people overcome learning problems. Students do better in schools where they feel welcomed and safe. They do best in environments where they feel connected to others, not in settings dominated by threat and fear. Harm reduction reverses the coercive or criminal justice approach to addictive behavior. Rather than try to remove a person's primary coping mechanisms until others are in place, harm reduction allows people to learn new skills before they move away from addiction. In many cases, particularly among the most traumatized and disenfranchised, this may be the only path to recovery.

The fundamental principles of harm reduction are simple, yet controversial. Recognizing that people always have and probably always will consume addictive substances and practice addictive behavior, and that this makes them neither irrational or subhuman, harm reduction urges society to stop fighting drug use directly, working indirectly to find practical methods that reduce risk and minimize damage. Harm reduction believes that when addicted people start to be valued by others and not just condemned or shamed, they start to value themselves. This also helps individuals coping with trauma, providing a foundation for forgiveness and further growth. Harm reduction is the opposite of tough love; it is unconditional kindness.

Significantly, harm reduction is already being applied selectively in our society. This approach, the mainstay of alcohol policy in this country since the repeal of "prohibition" in 1933 and evident with the introduction of the "designated driver" in the early 1980s, targets drunk driving, not drinking. Together, media campaigns against drunk driving, stricter laws, and the designated driver concept produced one of the greatest successes in public behavioral health. Since the 1980s, the percentage of deaths associated with drunk driving has fallen from 53 percent in 1982 to 31 percent in 2013. During that period, the total number of drunk driving deaths in the United States has been cut in half, with help, certainly, from improved auto safety, mainly in the form of seat belt laws.[3]

However, unlike other countries, mostly in Europe, the United States has resisted applying harm reduction for other drugs. The results have been disastrous. Drug overdose has taken the lives of 300,000 Americans over the past fifteen years, and experts are predicting that the same number will die in the next five.[4] Some overdoses have been fueled by the latest synthetic opioid, carfentanil, an elephant sedative imported from China. Carfentanil is one hundred times stronger than fentanyl, which is twenty-five to fifty times stronger than heroin.

In 2013, New Zealand became the first country to embark on a new and unprecedented drug policy task, finding a way to test, approve, and then regulate safe recreational drugs. The idea behind New Zealand's 2013 Psychoactive Substance Act was not to make more drugs available, but rather to try to get safer ones to push out the more dangerous ones. Recognizing that humans are pleasure seeking and risk taking beings, that banning one drug allows more dangerous ones to take its place, and that countries cannot outlaw everything that gets people high or addicted (else alcohol, coffee, tobacco, and maybe spices, sex, skydiving, mountain climbing, skiing, and provocative music would soon join the list of banned products and activities), New Zealand's approach recognized that regulation offers better control than prohibition.

In a calculated risk, New Zealand's law allowed drugs that were already being sold without reported problems for at least three months to remain legal. To detect problems, the Psychoactive Substance Regulatory Authority (an FDA-like administration for recreational drugs) set up an online tracking system that allowed doctors and hospitals to report adverse events connected to any given product. As New Zealand's strategy to test and regulate low-risk recreational drugs makes use of the new understanding

3. Szalavitz, *Unbroken Brain*, 233.
4. Macy, *Dopesick*, 5.

of addiction as a learning disorder, it can inform future efforts. By selecting drugs with low risk of addiction for approval, such policies can encourage people to replace more harmful drugs with less harmful ones. By setting pricing through taxation and by regulating the location of sale, they can affect the context of drug use and greatly eliminate illegal sale and distribution.

Knowing that punishment is not an effective way to teach people with addiction to recover, is there an alternative? While the United States has remained silent on New Zealand's experiment, other nations are citing this program as a possible model to emulate. Portugal, for instance, has decriminalized drugs and diverted public monies from incarceration to treatment and job creation. In America, now that four states and Washington, D.C. are experimenting with marijuana legalization, these states, as well as New Zealand, Portugal, and Uruguay (which recently legalized marijuana on a national level), could provide examples of what works, and what does not.

## Questions for Discussion and Reflection

1. According to the Bible, what is the purpose of creation, and why are human beings on earth?

2. Explain how addiction to religion can turn "means of grace" such as scripture and sacraments into obstacles for growth and spiritual transformation.

3. Explain how grace and love are related.

4. Explain how grace is the foundation upon which all liberation rests.

5. Explain the difference between "cheap grace" and 'costly grace." What do Christians mean when they claim, "judgment is covered by grace"?

6. Explain and assess the concept of the three incarnations of God.

7. Explain the meaning of the paradoxical statement, "Grace rarely means getting what we want, yet grace means always getting what we want."

8. In your estimation, is behavior change more likely to occur when harm reduction methods are used, or when punishment and other punitive means are used? Explain your answer.

9. In your estimation, what is the primary insight gained from this chapter?

10. *For personal reflection*: Does this chapter raise any issues you might need to address in the future?

# CHAPTER 12

# Awareness and Personality

The quest for the self and its deepest Essence culminates
in meeting the Divine.

—DON RICHARD RUSO AND RUSS HUDSON

IN OUR STUDY OF addiction, we must keep in mind that psychological
temperament—people's interpretations of their own experience, trauma,
and access to healthy ways of managing-distress—matters profoundly.
However, if the solution to the problems of life—whether in determining
national public policy or in discovering one's purpose in life—seems daunt-
ing, nebulous, or impractical, a good place to start the process of awareness
is with your own personality and story. Discovering your personality type,
and understanding how you have learned to cope, will shed significant light
on the nature of addiction, on how we get stuck and unstuck in our addictive patterns and behavior.

Human beings are graciously different; no two are alike. While each of
us can be typed psychologically, we are all distinguished by our individual
stories, how past experiences shape our identity, and how our identity influences our potential future. When we speak of personality, what do we
mean, and how does personality typing help us in our struggle against addiction? These questions drive our discussion in this chapter and close our
study of addictive behavior.

There is in every human an impetus which, when nourished, seeks health and wholeness. Physically, emotionally, and cognitively, we are designed for growth. Spiritually, we are designed for transformation. Our happiness is dependent upon growth, upon actualizing our potential. That truth was affirmed by ancient philosophers such as Plato and Aristotle and refined spiritually by medieval Christian theologians such as Augustine and Aquinas.

Grace has endowed us with the physical and spiritual potential for growth, but also with an innate longing for God. As Augustine stated in the famous passage from the *Confessions*: "You have made us for Yourself, and our hearts are restless until they find rest in You."

By now it should be clear that the character of God, indeed that the nature of reality, is gracious, loving, and compassionate. God (whether called Father, the Infinite, the Tao, Brahman, or Being) is life-giving and life-affirming, willing our transformation and the transformation of the world and involved in those transformations. The words gracious, loving, and compassionate are virtually synonymous in the Bible. We did not create ourselves; we are not self-made. Ultimately, all we are and have are gifts.

To say that God loves the world (John 3:16) means that God wills our well-being and the well-being of all creation. In the story of creation, found in the first chapter of Genesis, the account of each day of creation is followed by a divine affirmation of the goodness of what has been created. Because of the tendency of humans to fall short of their God-given potential, a deeper life with God is offered. On our part, such a relation must be intentional, meaning we must desire a deepening relationship with this powerful and all-loving reality. The image of the Christian life that goes with this view of God is quite different from the legalistic approach so many people take. Rather than placing additional duties and requirements upon us, the Christian life is about a relationship with God that transforms us into more compassionate beings. This is another way to speak of the grace of God.

When I began teaching courses on spirituality, I discovered the Myers-Briggs Type Indicator (MBTI) to be both insightful and useful. Based on the findings of the influential Swiss psychiatrist Carl Jung, the MBTI is a sorting device that reports individual preferences on four scales, each consisting of two opposite poles. Discovering my MBTI personality type changed the way I understood myself and others, and it became a valuable tool for use with college students, in church settings, and with adults in Special Studies courses at Chautauqua Institution.

At Chautauqua I became acquainted with another model for self-understanding and growth called the Enneagram (pronounced ANY-a-gram). Learning about the Enneagram significantly deepened my understanding of personality, particularly in its application to addictive patterns and behavior. The Enneagram is particularly germane to our subject because it provides a valuable map that guides us to the points of blockage in our particularly personality structures. If, as we have learned, addictive behaviors are maladjusted coping mechanisms, the Enneagram helps us understand how we learn to cope, how and why we close down and become constricted in our growth. It provides insights that can help free us from inner fears and conflicts, wayward passions and compulsions, and from disordered desires and inner confusions. In addition, the Enneagram offers answers to our spiritual needs because it show us with great specificity how our personality has limited us, what our path of growth is, and where real fulfillment can be found.

Because of their insightful contributions and transformative power, we will examine both approaches to personality theory in this chapter, beginning with the Jungian model, as revised in the 1940s by Isabel Briggs Myers and her mother, Katherine Cook Briggs.

## The Myers-Briggs Type Indicator[1]

If you have never taken the Myers Briggs Type Indicator (MBTI), or if you need to verify your personality type, I recommend that you take the online version of the test.[2] However, before you do, keep in mind that the MBTI is not really a test but a sorter of preferences. There is no "right" or "wrong" answer. In order to get accurate results, you need to remember that you are attempting to discover your preferred answer to each question, not what you or your parents or anyone else wished you preferred as an answer. Since

1. Portions of the segment on the MBTI are adapted from my earlier volume, *Iron Sharpens Iron*, 81–87.

2. To find your type, go to www.humanmetrics.com and click on "Jung Typology Test" and then "Take Test." Either before or after taking the test, click on the Full Description link for clarification of the Jungian terminology and concepts. Once you have completed the 72 questions, click "Score It" at the bottom to obtain your results. The entire exercise will take 10 to 15 minutes. For further analysis and potential verification of your personality type, consult www.personalitypathways.com/type-inventory.html.

humans are complex individuals, our preferences may vary from situation to situation.

At the conclusion of the test you will receive four letters, which comprise your personality type. They indicate the differences in people that result from

- where they prefer to focus their attention (Extraversion or Introversion)—E or I;
- the way they prefer to take in information (Sensing or Intuition)—S or N;
- the way they prefer to make decisions (Thinking or Feeling)—T or F;
- how they orient themselves to the external world (Judging or Perceiving) J or P.

These preferences produce sixteen different kinds of people, interested in different things and drawn to different fields. Each type has its own inherent strengths as well as its likely blind spots. Discovering one's personality type is extremely beneficial, for it influences career choices, marriage choices, learning style, spiritual journeys, theological understanding, and much more.

Using combinations of preferences yields interesting results on the topic of learning styles. Combining the first two letters of your type reveals some interesting patterns. The first two letters show where you prefer to focus your attention and how you prefer to take in information. For example, ES types are usually more interested in the practical usefulness of learning, while IN types are usually more interested in abstractions and learning for its own sake. Using the second and last letters of one's type is also a useful way to think about learning style. The second letter (S or N) describes whether one prefers to focus on facts and reality (Sensing) or abstract concepts and theories (Intuition). The last letter (J or P) indicates whether one prefers to decide on that information quickly and then move on (Judging) or keep open to new information (Perceiving).

Building on the insights of psychological type theory developed by Carl Jung and Isabel Briggs Myer, Peter Tufts Richardson notes that four different approaches to human spirituality emerge from the MBTI.[3] How we perceive the world and how we respond to it (how we judge) seems to be directly connected to the spiritual path we find most personally satisfying.

3. His approach is described in *Four Spiritualities*.

Utilizing the principle that one's spirituality flows out of one's individuality, Richardson locates the key to spirituality in the two middle letters of one's personality type. These cognitive pairs result in four possibilities: ST, SF, NT, and NF. One of these pairs defines each person's spirituality.

STs, for example, are characterized by a *task-oriented spirituality*. ST youth are drawn to activities that are task-oriented, such as team sports. And often they will be leaders. They may help with chores around the house, but they are not particularly swayed by the desires of a parent. They learn by experience, wanting to discover things for themselves; they need to know why things are required and how they work. As teens STs divide into two groups: the freedom lovers (STPs) and the responsible ones (STJs), but all are oriented around well-defined institutions. When they grow up, STs become the realists, always in touch with the facts, unbiased, objective, accurate, paying attention to relevant details. They are skilled administrators, responsible, consistent, efficient, and analytical. The Journey of Works is practical and involves a lifetime of effort; people on this path like to follow procedures efficiently, often legalistically. Work is the means for meeting all obligations and responsibilities. It gives life dignity and results in solid citizenship. STs commit themselves to the building up and maintaining of institutions, reliably and loyally. They prefer direct, experience-based, often physical activities, working with their hands or otherwise directly in situations, trying out procedures to see what works best, often preferring technical tasks to those requiring people skills. They learn best on the job, noticing relevant details, collecting facts, and verifying them directly by the senses. They arrive at conclusions in a linear cause-and-effect way. Their opinions, based on their experience, will often be firmly held and based on common sense. A confusion of beliefs is intolerable for STs. They like to find a world in balance, with reliable structures that lead them toward the right way to go. For the Journey of Works, order and a clear message are essential conditions. Appreciating clear beliefs and reliable structure, they tend to be literalists and legalists in religion; commitment provides religion stability.

SFs are characterized by an *experience-based spirituality*. SF youth make friends easily, avoid conflict, and desire to please. They thrive in well-structured environments and when expectations are clear. They need to be reassured when they are on the right track and rewarded for good behavior. As adults SFs are sensitive, loyal, and caring; they live responsibly as parents and citizens and are devoted to serving others in tangible ways. In the

Journey of Devotion, living in the immediate present is central. Instead of the cosmic, the tangible task at hand is the focus. Details are important. Stressing continuity and propriety, SFs are traditionalists. In their communications they prefer anecdotes, stories, and tangible references to symbolic or abstract reasoning. Practical and interactive, they take a tactile, hands-on approach to the spiritual life.

NTs are characterized by a *highly principled spirituality*. NT youth value their independence and tend to work hard to establish their competence in the challenges they decide to tackle. Uncomfortable with abstraction, they often ask why, and if the answers they receive are unsatisfactory, they may set out to improve upon them or else to rebel against arbitrary answers. As adults NTs tend to enjoy solving problems, love to exchange ideas, or stimulate new efforts. Searching for unifying solutions, they appreciate speculative theories that lead to intellectual clarity. In the Journey of Unity, the search for truth or the quest for perfection is often as satisfying as the conclusions reached along the way. NTs are foremost change agents and strategic planners. On account of their critical nature, they may be perceived by others, particularly SFs, as stubborn or uncooperative. Along with principles and truth, individuals on this path are also distinguished by vision and concern for social justice.

NFs are characterized by a *questing spirituality*. NF youth like to please the adults and peers in their lives. They can be easily crushed by disapproval or even indifference. They need regular affirmation from parents and teachers if their self-esteem and self-image are not to suffer. Because they see possibilities in the future (N) and like to gain approval from others, they often will prepare for careers and causes in response to adult mentors in their lives. NF youth are exceedingly idealistic. Their idealism is often unpredictable; some young men may overcompensate for their F by expressing their idealism in hostile ways. They are strongly represented among protestors for social issues. NF adults are enthusiastic and insightful, recognizing the personal needs of others. Idealists by nature, they always see a way to make life better. They have an ability to draw people into a discussion and to facilitate consensus-building for social harmony and good. NFs on a healthy track will regularly draw others toward their own best selves. The Intuitive proclivity for symbol and metaphor, combining with global vision for the well-being of the world, makes NFs inspired communicators of the ideal. Future-oriented and attuned to the big picture of life as a whole, people on the Journey of Harmony tend to focus more on possibilities than on concrete situations at hand. Their N nature is balanced, however, by their F side, which keeps them in touch with reality and keeps their utopian bent in check. Flexible and open to change, NFs see life as continual self-creating process, a quest toward selfhood. Their malleable natures exist to be formed and re-formed in ever more exquisite patterns of self-actualization. NFs seek increasing meaning and spiritual purpose in life.

## The Enneagram[4]

As with the MBTI, if you do not know your Enneagram type or number, or if you need to verify your personality type, there are numerous online versions of the test. While some are free, I recommend that you take a version designed by Don Riso and Richard Hudson, either online or one found in their writings. Initial results may be confusing, for you will discover traits in your personality common to various personality types. This is not erroneous, for in actuality each person possesses the entire Enneagram in his or her psyche. You may need to take various forms of the Enneagram test, perhaps even more than once, until you receive clarity.

Once you get consistent results, make sure they reveal not only your type but also your "wing." In the Enneagram, as in life, there are no pure types. Types should not be viewed as single points along the circumference of a circle, but rather as a range of points crystallized somewhere on that circumference Everyone is a unique mixture of one's basic type and one of the two types adjacent to it, called a "wing." Next in importance to the basic type, the auxiliary type, or wing, provides the basic type with important psychological functions, sometimes complementing the basic type, sometimes working in opposition to it. While the vast majority of people seem to have a dominant wing, some individuals seem to have either wings or no wing.

One of the most challenging notions for us to accept initially about integrative work is that personality—the ego and its structures—is an artificial construct.[5] Until now, our personality seems to have been our entire reality. Identifying with our personality has been how we have lived and

4. Portions of the segment on the Enneagram are adapted from my earlier volume, *Living Graciously on Planet Earth*, 110–22.

5. While psychological and spiritual growth go together, they are distinct. Hence, this chapter uses "integration" to describe psychological work and "transformation" to describe spiritual work.

gotten by in life. But as we examine our personality more objectively, we realize that it consists largely of a collection of internal defenses and reactions, deeply ingrained beliefs and habits about the self and the world that have come from the past, particularly from our childhood. In the past our personality has helped us cope and survive, but upon adult reflection, we see its limitation. This personality has served as a mask, creating both a mistaken identity and an illusion of permanence.

If there is a theme to the Enneagram, or a lesson to be learned by studying personality types, it is that while humans legitimately look for happiness by seeking personal fulfillment, they often seek it wrongly. As humans look for happiness, each personality type creates a self-fulfilling prophecy, bringing about the very thing it most fears while losing what it most desires. In most cases, the personality creates survival techniques such as anger, resentment, shame, and envy as protective mechanisms for the ego, but in the process, these attitudes hide or cover our spiritual core. In addition, the painful events of early childhood create certain ways of interpreting our experiences, so that later life events reinforce our beliefs about our self and our world. As a result of this reinforcement of our earliest sense of self, our personality thickens, perpetuating certain patterns around which our identity revolves.

The personality is highly automatic, and it leads us into repetitive patterns and problems. But the personality is only automatic when we are not aware of it. With awareness come power, wisdom, energy, and strength. Learning to let go of the protective patterns of our personality enables us to be more present and awake, more energized and alive.

According to the Enneagram, inner integrative work proceeds layer by layer, from the most external forms of personality to the inner core of our being. The automatic pattern of our personality draws us outward, but by bringing awareness to these patterns, we can reverse the course. Willing to know the truth about what is really occurring in us dissolves the structures in which we are trapped.

The Enneagram encourages us to become aware of our personality type, including our strengths and weaknesses (virtues and vices), and provides discernable stages for growth. According to medieval Christian thinking, humans are tempted by seven deadly sins: lust, gluttony, greed, sloth, anger, envy, and pride. To defeat the seven deadly vices, Christians were encouraged to practice seven heavenly virtues, identified as chastity, abstinence, liberality, diligence, patience, kindness, and humility. Adding two vices (deceit and fear) to the traditional notion of the Seven Deadly Sins, the Enneagram identifies nine "Passions" or root sins: Anger, Pride, Deceit, Envy, Avarice (greed), Fear, Gluttony, Lust, and Sloth. These traps or obsessions represent our primary emotional compulsions or mistaken attitudes, nine main ways that we lose our center and become distorted in our thinking, feeling, and doing.

For those unfamiliar with the Enneagram or who wish additional information, the following segment describes the nine personality types, including their primary virtues and vices (Passions).[6] As you examine the nine types, you need to know that Don Riso and Russ Hudson identified nine stages or Levels of Development within each type, constituting a continuum of interrelated traits running from healthy (levels 1–3) to average (levels 4–6) to unhealthy states (levels 7–9).

**Type One**: *The Perfectionist* (Reformer)—*The Need to be Perfect*. Ones are ethical and conscientious, with a strong sense of right and wrong. Their primary virtue is *Prudence*, sobriety, or objectivity. They are teachers and crusaders, always striving to improve things but afraid of making a mistake. Well-organized, orderly, and fastidious, they try to maintain high standards but can slip into being critical and perfectionistic. Their primary Passion is *Anger*, not overt anger, but repressed anger, leading to frustration, impatience, and dissatisfaction with themselves and with the world. At their best, healthy Ones are wise, discerning, realistic, and noble, as well as morally heroic. Unhealthy Ones tend to be dogmatic, inflexible, opinionated, judgmental self-righteous condemning and compulsive. Feeling they alone know "the truth," they can become intolerant and inflexible. Behind the scenes, however, unhealthy Ones are bitter and depressed, compulsively acting out of "forbidden pleasures." Obsessed about the wrongdoings of others, they may do the same thing or worse themselves. They may become condemnatory of others, punitive and cruel to rid themselves of "wrongdoers." Believing themselves partly responsible for their suffering can result in self-punishment or self-mutilation.

**Type Two**: *The Helper* (Giver)—*The Need to be Needed*. Twos are empathetic, sincere, and warm-hearted. Their primary virtue is *Humility*. They are friendly, generous, and self-sacrificing, but they can also be sentimental, flattering, and people-pleasing. They are driven to be close to others, and they often do things for others in order to be needed. They typically have

6. Riso and Hudson, *Wisdom of the Enneagram*, 11–12, 23, 97–340; see also *Personality Types*.

problems taking care of themselves and acknowledging their own needs. Their primary Passion is *Pride*, better described as Vainglory—pride in their own virtue. At their best, healthy Twos are unselfish and altruistic and have unconditional love for themselves and others. Unhealthy Twos tend to be self-serving, resentful, manipulative, possessive, coercive, victimized, and entitled. Feeling unwanted and unappreciated, unhealthy Twos may abuse food and medication to get sympathy. Obsessive love and stalking can occur. Repressed anger becomes evident in psychosomatic problems.

**Type Three:** *The Achiever* (Performer)—*The Need to Succeed.* Threes are self-assured, attractive, and charming. Their primary virtue is *Truthfulness*. Ambitious, competent, and energetic, they can also be status-conscious and highly driven for personal advancement. Threes are often concerned about their image and what others think of them. They typically have problems with workaholism and competitiveness. Their primary passion is *Vanity* or deceit, putting effort into developing their ego instead of their true nature. At their best, healthy Threes are self-accepting, authentic, and everything they seem to be—role models who inspire others. Unhealthy Threes tend to be narcissistic, exhibitionist, vindictive, exploitative, deceptive, and career-addicted. Unable to deal with emotional turmoil, they bury it beneath a functional façade. Relying on self-deception, they can resort to false resumes, plagiarism, and other forms of dishonesty.

**Type Four:** *The Individualist* (Romantic)—*The Need to be Special.* Fours are self-aware, sensitive, reserved, and quiet. Their primary virtue is *Self-Control.* They are self-revealing, emotionally honest, and personal, but they can also be moody and self-conscious. Withholding themselves from others due to feeling vulnerable and defective, they can also feel disdainful and exempt from ordinary ways of living. They typically have problems with self-indulgence and self-pity. Their primary Passion is *Envy*, feeling that others possess qualities that they lack. At their best, healthy Fours are inspired and highly creative, able to renew themselves and transform their experiences. Unhealthy Fours tend to be moody, narcissistic, hypersensitive, self-indulgent, despairing, decadent, alienated, and depressed. As ideas about themselves become more unrealistic, they tend to reject anyone or anything in their life that does not support their self-image. Feeling worthless and hopeless, they despair and become self-destructive, possibly abusing alcohol or drugs to escape their self-hatred.

**Type Five:** *The Investigator* (Observer)—*The Need to Perceive.* Fives are alert, insightful, and curious. Their primary virtue is *Detachment.* They are able to concentrate and focus on developing complex ideas and skills. Independent and innovative, they can become preoccupied with their thoughts and imaginary constructs. They become detached, yet high-strung and intense. They typically have problems with isolation, eccentricity, and nihilism. Their primary Passion is *Avarice*. At their best, healthy Fives are visionary pioneers, often ahead of their time and able to see the world in an entirely new way. Rejecting all social attachment, unhealthy Fives tend to be reclusive, isolated, scornful, eccentric, nihilistic, dissociative, and delusional. Fearful of aggression from others, they become increasingly suspicious and emotionally overwrought.

**Type Six:** *The Loyalist* (Critic)—*The Need for Security.* Sixes are reliable, hardworking, and responsible, but they can also be defensive, evasive, and highly anxious—running on stress while complaining about it. Their primary virtue is *Courage*. They are often cautious and indecisive but can also be reactive, defiant, and rebellious. They typically have problems with self-doubt and suspicion. Their primary Passion is *Fear* or anxiety about possible future events. At their best, healthy Sixes are internally stable, self-confident, and self-reliant, courageously supporting the weak and powerless. Unhealthy Sixes tend to be unreliable, evasive, self-doubting, paranoid, aggressive, panicky, and cowardly. Fearing they have ruined their security either by impulsive acts of defiance or by lack of initiative, they become highly insecure. They may look to others for rescue or become loners who seek relief from anxieties in fanatical beliefs or in substance abuse.

**Type Seven:** *The Enthusiast* (Epicurean)—*The Need to Avoid Pain.* Sevens are versatile, optimistic, and spontaneous. Their primary virtue is *Temperance* or moderation. Playful, high-spirited, and practical, they can also be overextended, scattered, and undisciplined. They constantly seek new and exciting experiences, but they can become distracted and exhausted by staying on the go. They typically have problems with superficiality and impulsiveness. Their primary Passion is *Gluttony* or intemperance, feeling that they never have enough. At their best, healthy Sevens focus their talents on worthwhile goals, becoming joyous, highly accomplished, and full of gratitude. Unhealthy Sevens tend to be unfocused, impetuous, excessive, reckless, and panic-stricken. Desperate to suppress their anxieties, they are easily frustrated, becoming rude and abusive as they demand whatever it is they believe they need to keep their panic under control. Increasingly hardened by their lavishness and excesses, yet unsatisfied, they begin to lose the capacity for pleasure, or to feel anything. Terrified by their inner chaos, they act out impulses rather than dealing with anxiety, going out of control, prey to erratic mood swings and compulsive actions. They engage in wild sprees, as if there are no limits. Physical disabilities from excessive lifestyle are common.

**Type Eight:** *The Challenger* (Protector)—*The Need to be Against*. Eights are self-confident, strong, and assertive. Their primary virtue is *Justice* or innocence. Protective, resourceful, and decisive, they can also be proud and domineering. Eights feel that they must control their environment, often becoming confrontational and intimidating. They typically have problems with allowing themselves to be close to others. Their primary Passion is *Lust* or need for control. At their best, healthy Eights are self-mastering—they use their strength to improve others' lives, becoming heroic, magnanimous, and sometimes historically great. Unhealthy Eights tend to be proud, egocentric, defiant, vengeful, domineering, violent, destructive, and tyrannical. They feel deeply betrayed, but also feel that they have crossed some limit and cannot go back. Defying any attempt to control them, they develop an outlaw mentality, respecting no law or limit on their behavior. Some become criminals, renegades, and con-artists.

**Type Nine:** *The Peacemaker* (Mediator)—*The Need to Avoid*. Nines are accepting, trusting, and stable. Their primary virtue is *Fortitude* or emotional stability. They are good-natured, kind-hearted, easygoing, and supportive but can also be too willing to go along with others to keep the peace. They want everything to be without conflict but can tend to be complacent and minimize anything upsetting. They typically have problems with passivity and stubbornness. Their primary Passion is *Sloth*, not as in laziness, but in their desire to be unaffected by life. At their best, healthy Nines are indomitable and all-embracing; they are able to bring people together and heal conflicts. Unhealthy Nines tend to be disengaged, unreflective, irresponsible, stubborn, resentful, fatalistic, and disoriented. Sitting on top of enormous unexpressed rage, they can become highly depressed, seriously neglectful and dangerous to anyone who needs them.

## Type Dynamics

Some people question whether it is possible to change one's basic personality type, especially as one gets older. While people develop throughout life, they do not change from one personality to another, but rather remain their type for life. They grow or deteriorate from that beginning point—their basic type—which reflects who they became as the result of genetics, parenting, and other childhood experiences, The purpose of the Enneagram is not to help people get rid of their personality, but rather to help people utilize their personality to recognize that it is only a small part of the totality of who they are. The Enneagram provides access to the wisdom we need to let go of the limiting mechanisms of our personality so that we can more deeply experience our essential self.

The mechanism of the personality is set in motion by what we call the *Basic Fear* of each type.[7] This fear arises during early childhood. As the result of unmet infant needs and subsequent blockages, we inevitably conclude that there is something wrong with us; this unconscious anxiety is called our Basic Fear. While we can recognize the Basic Fears of all nine types in ourselves, our own type's Basic Fear motivates our behavior more than the others. Unfortunately, as the following examples illustrate, the agendas of our egos are ultimately self-defeating:

*Ones* strive to maintain personal integrity but still feel divided and at war with themselves.

*Twos* spend their lives searching for love from others and still feel that they are unloved.

*Threes* pursue achievement and recognition but still feel worthless and empty.

*Fours* spend their lives trying to discover the meaning of their personal identity and still do not know who they are.

*Fives* accumulate knowledge and skills and build up their confidence but still feel helpless and incapable.

*Sixes* toil to create security for themselves and still feel anxious and fearful about the world.

*Sevens* look high and low for happiness but still feel unhappy and frustrated.

*Eights* do everything in their power to protect themselves and their interests but still feel vulnerable and threatened.

*Nines* sacrifice a great deal to achieve inner peace and stability but still feel ungrounded and insecure.

7. Riso and Hudson., *Wisdom of the Enneagram*, 30-33

When we examine the average or normal range of each type, we discover a social role, the need we feel to be a certain way, and the way we need other people to respond to us as being that way. To compensate for these needs, we become much more dependent on the particular coping mechanisms of our type, and we tend to be more fixated on achieving our Basic Desire through these mechanisms. Observing yourself as you slip in and out of your type's social role is a powerful and practical way to make life your arena for transformational practice. Here is a listed of manipulative efforts by type:[8]

Type One: by correcting others, by insisting that others share their standards.

Type Two: by finding out others' needs and desires, thus creating dependencies.

Type Three: by charming others and by adopting whatever image "works."

Type Four: by being temperamental, and making others "walk on eggshells."

Type Five: by staying preoccupied, and by detaching emotionally from others.

Type Six: by complaining, and by testing others' commitments to them.

Type Seven: By distracting others, and by insisting that others meet their demands.

Type Eight: by dominating others, and by demanding that others do as they say.

Type Nine: by "checking out," and by passive-aggressively resisting others.

To compensate for the Basic Fear, a *Basic Desire* arises. The Basic Desire is the way we defend against our Basic Fear in order to continue to function. The Basic Desire is what we believe will make us okay. The Basic Desire may be called the ego agenda, because it tells us what the ego self is striving after. Thus we might say that the whole of personality structure is composed of our flight from our Basic Fear and our single-minded pursuit of our Basic Desire, as the following examples illustrate.

Type One: the desire to have integrity (deteriorates into critical perfectionism)

8. Ibid., 81.

Type Two: the desire to be loved (deteriorates into the need to be needed)

Type Three: the desire to be valuable (deteriorates into chasing after success)

Type Four: the desire to be oneself (deteriorates into self-indulgence)

Type Five: the desire to be competent (deteriorates into useless specialization)

Type Six: the desire to be secure (deteriorates into an attachment to beliefs)

Type Seven: the desire to be happy (deteriorates into frenetic escapism)

Type Eight: the desire to protect oneself (deteriorates into constant fighting)

Type Nine: the desire to be at peace (deteriorates into stubborn neglectfulness)[9]

According to the Enneagram, if we are to find happiness, we must let go of the familiar and embrace the unfamiliar. People in the healthy range are able to move in their Direction of Integration (toward self-actualization, letting go of old habitual patterns and moving toward a richer, fuller life), while those in the average to unhealthy range "act out" in the Direction of Disintegration ("their path of least resistance").

Under conditions of increased stress and anxiety, types in their average to unhealthy range of behavior will begin to exhibit or "act out" some of the average or unhealthy behaviors of the type in their *Direction of Disintegration*. A person tends to act out of the behavior in the type in his or her Direction of Disintegration at roughly the same level at which they are functioning in their own type:

Methodical Ones become moody and irrational as average or unhealthy Fours;

Needy Twos become aggressive and dominating as average or unhealthy Eights;

Driven Threes become disengaged and apathetic as average or unhealthy Nines;

Aloof Fours become overinvolved and clinging as average or unhealthy Twos;

9. Ibid., 33.

Detached Fives become hyperactive and scattered as average or unhealthy Sevens;

Dutiful Sixes become competitive and arrogant as average or unhealthy Threes;

Scattered Sevens become perfectionistic and critical as average or unhealthy Ones;

Self-confident Eights become secretive and fearful as average or unhealthy Fives;

Complacent Nines become anxious and worried as average or unhealthy Sixes.[10]

The Direction of Disintegration is said to be unconscious and compulsive (the ego's way of automatically compensating for psychic imbalance), while moving in the Direction of Integration requires conscious choice. When we are on the path of integration, we are saying to ourselves: "I want to grow and be happy, and to do so, I must live intentionally." As we become familiar with our inner baggage, the very qualities we need for growth become accessible to us, speeding the progress of liberation from the patterns of our personality.

In a sense, one can think of each personality type as flowing into another, marking a further development of the prior type, much as the Direction of Disintegration marks a type's further entanglement in conflicted ego states. The *Direction of Integration* is a natural outgrowth of the healthiest qualities of that type.

*Ones* need to overcome their criticality and rigidity by moving toward the joy and enthusiasm of healthy *Sevens*.

*Twos* need to overcome their tendency to deceive themselves about their need, feelings, and motives by moving toward the self-understanding and emotional honesty of healthy *Fours*.

*Threes* need to overcome their desire to surpass others and draw attention to themselves by moving toward the commitment and humility of healthy *Sixes*.

*Fours* need to overcome their moodiness and self-indulgence by moving toward the integrity and self-discipline of healthy *Ones*.

10. Ibid., 89.

*Fives* need to overcome their detachment and cynicism by moving toward the practicality and courage of healthy *Eights*.

*Sixes* need to overcome their pessimism and suspicion of others by moving toward the hopefulness and receptivity of healthy *Nines*.

*Sevens* need to overcome their superficiality and impulsiveness by moving toward the depth and focus of healthy *Fives*.

*Eights* need to overcome their emotional armoring and egocentricity by moving toward the compassion and concern for others of healthy *Twos*.

*Nines* need to overcome their complacency and self-forgetting by moving toward the energy and self-investment of healthy *Threes*.[11]

Ultimately, the goal is to move completely around the Enneagram, integrating what each type symbolizes and acquiring the active use of the healthy potentials of all the types. The ideal is to become a balanced, fully functioning human being, and each of the types symbolizes a different important aspect of what we need to achieve this end. Utilizing the Enneagram as a spiritual tool, Riso and Hudson have developed "the Enneagram of Letting Go," a nine-step pattern for letting go of troublesome habits or defensive patterns.[12] Whether you follow the Direction of Integration or develop your own use of the Enneagram, the diagram's use as a transformative tool is practically limitless.

The qualities or virtues associated with the Enneagram personality types are among the most important payoffs we get for working on ourselves. The ego or false self does not naturally possess any of these virtues, for they represent the opposite of the state we are in ordinarily when we identify with our personality. However, when we become aware of these blockages to our true Self, the virtues start emerging spontaneously and become available as they are needed. We need do nothing but let go of the attachment.

11. Ibid., 92.
12. Ibid., 363–66.

# Addiction and the Types[13]

If someone is stuck in an addictive pattern or actively abusing medications, alcohol, or other harmful substances, the transformational work we are discussing will not be possible. If you have a substance abuse or addictive behavioral problem, you must become "sober" or let go of the addictive behavior before you can sustain in-depth inquiry into your true nature. All nine types can have any kind of addiction, of course, and all nine types can be codependent. However, tendencies towards addiction can be associated with each type. The following examples feature addictions associated with food, body, drugs, and other physical imbalance.

Type One: Excessive use of diets, vitamins, and cleansing techniques; undereating for self-control; alcohol to relieve tension.

Type Two: Abusing food and over-the-counter medications; bingeing, especially on sweets and carbohydrates; hypochondria to look for sympathy.

Type Three: Overstressing the body for recognition; working out to exhaustion; starvation diets; workaholism; excessive intake of coffee, stimulants, amphetamines, cocaine, or steroids, or excessive surgery for cosmetic improvement.

Type Four: Overindulgence in rich foods and sweets; use of alcohol to alter mood, to socialize, and for emotional consolation; lack of physical activity; bulimia; depression; tobacco, prescription drugs, or heroin for social anxiety; cosmetic surgery to erase rejected features.

Type Five: Poor eating and sleeping habits due to minimizing needs; neglect of hygiene and nutrition; lack of physical activity; psychotropic drugs for mental stimulation and escape, and narcotics and alcohol for anxiety.

Type Six: Rigidity in diet causes nutritional imbalances; working excessively; caffeine and amphetamines for stamina, but also alcohol and depressants to deaden anxiety; higher susceptibility to alcoholism than most types.

Type Seven: The type most prone to addiction; stimulants (caffeine, cocaine, and amphetamines); ecstasy, psychotropics, narcotics, and

13. Ibid., 351.

alcohol; tendency to avoid depressants; consumerism and compulsive shopping; fatiguing the body; excessive cosmetic surgery; painkillers.

Type Eight: Ignoring physical needs and problems; avoiding medical visits and checkups; indulging in rich food, alcohol, and tobacco while pushing self too hard, leading to high stress, stroke, and heart condition; control issues are central, although alcoholism and narcotic addictions are possible.

Type Nine: Overeating or undereating due to lack of self-awareness and repressed anger; lack of physical activity; depressants and psychotropics, alcohol, marijuana, and narcotics to deaden loneliness and anxiety.

## Healing and the Types

Thankfully, many resources are available to support us in breaking free of addiction, including books, workshops, support groups, therapy, and in-patient care. The Enneagram is not intended to be a substitute for those resources, but combined with them, it can be extremely helpful in understanding the roots of addictive patterns. The following healing attitudes are associated with particular types.[14]

Type One. Maybe others are right. Maybe someone else has a better idea. Maybe others will learn for themselves. Maybe I've done all that can be done.

Type Two. Maybe I could let someone else do this. Maybe this person is actually already showing me love in his or her own way. Maybe I could do something good for myself, too.

Type Three. Maybe I don't have to be the best. Maybe people will accept me just the way I am. Maybe others' opinions of me aren't so important.

Type Four. Maybe there's nothing wrong with me. Maybe others do understand me and support me. Maybe I'm not the only one who feels this way.

Type Five. Maybe I can trust people and let them know what I need. Maybe I can live happily in the world. Maybe my future will be okay.

14. Ibid., 355.

Type Six. Maybe this will work out fine. Maybe I don't have to foresee every possible problem. Maybe I can trust myself and my own judgments.

Type Seven. Maybe what I already have is enough. Maybe there's nowhere else I need to be right now. Maybe I'm not missing out on anything worthwhile.

Type Eight. Maybe this person isn't out to take advantage of me. Maybe I can let down my guard a little more. Maybe I could let my heart be touched more deeply.

Type Nine. Maybe I can make a difference. Maybe I need to get energized and be involved. Maybe I am more powerful than I realize.

According to Enneagram theory, the nine personality types are not isolated categories but are interrelated in profound ways. The human psyche, thus understood, can be divided into Triads, different groups of three. The Triads are important for integrative work because they specify where our chief imbalance lies. The Triads represent the three main clusters of issues and defenses of the ego—instinct, feeling, and thinking—and they reveal the principal ways by which humans limit themselves. These three functions are related to "Centers" in the human body, and the personality fixation is associated primarily in one of these Centers.[15]

- *The Instinctive Triad*: Types Eight, Nine, and One are concerned with maintaining resistance to reality (creating boundaries for the self that are based on physical tensions). These types tend to have problems with aggression and repression. Underneath their ego defenses they carry a great deal of *rage*.

- *The Feeling Triad*: Types Two, Three, and Four are concerned with self-image (attachment to the false or assumed self of personality). They believe that the stories about themselves and their assumed qualities are their actual identity. Underneath their ego defenses these types carry a great deal of *shame*.

- *The Thinking Triad*: Types Five, Six, and Seven are concerned with anxiety (they experience a lack of support and guidance). They engage in behaviors that they believe will enhance their safety and security. Underneath their ego defenses these types carry a great deal of *fear*.

15. Ibid, 51.

All integrative work begins with the body. It is important not only because it houses our minds and emotions, but because it provides a reality check for the other two centers. While our minds and feelings may be anywhere—fantasizing the present, imaging the future, dwelling on the past—the body is always here, in the present moment. If we are to make progress in life, we must take care of our bodies. A good place to start is with a good diet, frequent exercise, and proper rest. Good health is central to psychological and spiritual growth. When we eat sensibly and get sufficient exercise and rest, our emotions are steadier and our minds are clearer, enabling growth and integration to proceed smoothly.

Physical health should be accompanied by mental health, and the best place to start mentally is with a quiet mind. Silence, achieved through meditation and contemplation, is essential to a calm and confidant mind. When the mind is at peace, it is grounded in the spirit or soul, one's inner being. Expansive awareness, as we noted in chapter 8, sustains the resolve necessary for spiritual growth. As we become more relaxed and aware, we understand that our normal condition is chaotic and unfocused, whereas the quiet mind adds qualities of sobriety, clarity, and steadiness. In short, when our minds become more still and silent, our awareness becomes aligned with a transcendent intelligence that understands our situation objectively and understands what we need to do or not do. When our senses are sharp, we are alert and attentive to everything around us and within us.

Finally, change and integration cannot occur without emotional wholeness, without healing the heart. If our heart is closed, no matter how much spiritual knowledge we have accumulated, we will not be able to respond to our deepest call. An open heart enables us to participate fully in our experiences and to connect in a real way with the people in our lives. True knowing emanates from the heart.

Healing the heart can be difficult because as we open it, we inevitably encounter our own pain and become more aware of the pain of others. In fact, our addictive patterns and behavior have been adopted because they help dull this suffering. However, shutting out our pain also renders us unable to feel joy, compassion, love, and the other capacities of the heart. Spiritual work, if it is to be transformative, must be confrontational. It neither provides pity or allow us to remain in denial. Despite its boldness, spiritual work is not designed to make us masochists; the idea is to transform our suffering, not to prolong it. We do not need to take on additional suffering; rather, we need to explore the roots of the suffering that we already have.

We need to look beneath the defenses of our personality to explore the fears and hurts that drive us. As we have noted, the more suffering we carry from our past, the more rigid and controlling our personality structures become, but they are not invincible. When we examine our personality naturally and honestly, including the traits and qualities we have created to cope and survive, we encounter considerable sadness and pain. This is when it is important to remember that unconditional love and grace underlie life, both as the motivating energy and as the end toward which we are drawn.

One of the most important elements of spiritual progress is the willingness and ability to let go of the past, and this inevitably means wrestling with the problem of forgiving those who have hurt us. Again, we cannot simply "decide" to forgive, any more than we can "decide" to be loving. Rather, love and forgiveness arise naturally when we let go of the old ego self and attach to the deity incarnated in our eternal Self.

The process of growth is evolutionary, not sudden, an upward spiral that has no final state of completion. If self-realization is thought of as merely collecting a set of impractical virtues as if they were merit badges added to a collection, then the process will be unsatisfying. The true situation is far different. Acquiring the strengths of virtue brings about the enlargement of the person. The creation of inner resources, the experience of oneself as enlarged, more potent, and creative is tremendously fulfilling. Transformation entails the surrender of nothing—our personality—in order to receive the gift of everything—the life of the Spirit. And nothing in life is more fulfilling than cooperating in the process of creation. Transformed people become co-creators of that vast yet intimate mystery, the human spirit.

From a psychological point of view, the capacity to be a co-creator bestows on human nature enormous dignity. However, "from a spiritual point of view, this capacity has a more profound meaning because to move in the direction of increasing life is to move toward Being itself. . . . In the end, the quest for the self and its deepest Essence culminates in meeting the Divine."[16]

## Questions for Discussion and Reflection

1. Discuss how discovering one's personality type sheds light on the nature of addiction and on the means of escape from addictive traps.

16. Riso and Hudson, *Understanding the Enneagram*, 381.

2. Do you know your Myers-Briggs personality type? If so, what do the four letters associated with your type tell you about your *personality*?

3. Do you know your Myers-Briggs personality type? If so, what do the four letters associated with your type tell you about your *spirituality*?

4. Do you know your Enneagram type or number? If so, what does it tell you about your personality?

5. Do you know your Enneagram type or number? If so, what does it tell you about your character strengths and weaknesses?

6. Do you know your Enneagram type or number? If so, what does it tell you about your healthy self and your unhealthy self?

7. Do you know your Enneagram type or number? If so, what does it tell you about your basic fears and manipulative efforts?

8. Do you know your Enneagram type or number? If so, what does it tell you about your basic desires?

9. Do you know your Enneagram type or number? If so, what does it tell you about your direction of integration (toward self-actualization) and direction of disintegration (the ego's unhealthy way to compensate for psychic imbalance)?

10. Do you know your Enneagram type or number? If so, what does it tell you about your tendencies toward addiction?

11. In your estimation, what is the primary insight gained from this chapter?

12. *For personal reflection*: Does this chapter raise any issues you might need to address in the future?

# Epilogue

*Celebrating Neurodiversity*

AS WE HAVE SEEN, trying to eliminate drug use and other forms of addictive behavior is futile. Fear-based prevention tends to deter those who wouldn't become addicted anyway, and it can actually make drugs more attractive to those who are looking for intense experiences or social acceptance. People will continue to find ways to alter their moods and behavior, so we can either accept this reality and try to reduce the damage, or aim for unrealistic ideals, regardless of the damage done while seeking it. When we look at the alternative, at the harm related to enforcement, incarceration, corruption, black-market-associated violence, the spread of disease, and the impure drug supplies that result from prohibition, we know there must be a better way.

Prevention efforts should focus more on teaching children to cope with their specific temperaments in healthier ways—and less on harmful substances. Such prevention should start early in life, helping kids understand their temperaments and their emotions and how to maximize self-control. We should also inform youth about labeling, and how it can influence people's sense of worth.

As we learn from the New Zealand model, it is cheaper and easier to regulate a market and control factors like price, places where recreational drug use is permitted, time when it is acceptable, and purity than it is to try to legislate and enforce drugs out of existence. Consequently, all drug policies need to be weighed as to whether they increase harm and make addiction more likely, or whether they decrease negative outcomes. One policy change that is widely supported by existing data is decriminalizing low-level possession and personal use of drugs. There may be drugs for which prohibitions of sales remains sensible, but this should not be the unquestioned default. People who use drugs also need access to accurate harm reduction information, and this includes high school and college students, who are most at risk. They need to know, for example, that mixing depressant drugs like alcohol with pain relievers can be deadly, but that there is no way to overdose on marijuana. Above all, science and research need to guide policy, not outdated, racially biased morality.

One of the intents of criminalization is to create stigma. If punishment accompanies treatment, addiction will remain the most stigmatized disorder in medicine. To get out of this loop, we need to regard addiction as a developmental disorder, one not inherently associated with dishonesty, cruelty, or harm to others. We also need to confront the racism that drives many aspects of drug policy—and ensure that selective enforcement becomes a thing of the past. Drug policy needs to be about reducing drug-related harm, not about sending political messages.

However, reducing stigma requires more than this. To increase acceptance of people with addictions and other developmental disorders, we cannot treat them as subhuman. Instead, we need to recognize and celebrate the differences people have in brain wiring, often indicative of strengths and abilities, not just disabilities. A movement aimed at celebrating "neurodiversity" is occurring among disability rights advocates fighting for civil rights of autistic people. The idea behind neurodiversity is that wiring differences—whether they produce autism, ADHD, or any other diagnosable condition—are just as deserving of respect as other human differences.[1]

In the same way that accommodations may be necessary for people with physical disabilities, so, too, society should work to adapt to the needs of people whose brains work in atypical ways. As The Good Doctor show on television demonstrates, when autistic people are allowed to act in ways that make them feel safe and comfortable, disabilities can often be significantly reduced. People should not be blamed for the way they are wired. We can either accept neurodiversity and foster a society where many types flourish or ignore diversity and marginalize people with disabilities. Moreover, just as people have strengths associated with their wiring, so, too, people with addictions. The autistic ability to focus on systems and ideas often leads to superior skills in music, math, and computer programming. The same brain that is vulnerable to overload in the wrong conditions can be superior to ordinary brains in the right ones.

1. Szalavitz, Unbroken Brain, 282–83.

Similarly, the ability to persist despite negative consequences, common in people with disabilities, can evoke admiration and success, not just compulsion and addiction. In fact, without persistence, few people with any kind of brain wiring, typical or atypical, would ever succeed as activists, artists, or entrepreneurs. Nor would anyone be able to sustain relationships and raise children. Setbacks, rejections, insults, and obstacles are part of life; few goals worth reaching exclude them.

When the compulsion and drive that get misguided during addiction is channeled in more positive directions, the results can be wonderful. We can all think of talented people in nearly every area of achievement who have experienced addictions, from William Steward Halsted, a founder of Johns Hopkins and surgeon whose techniques are still used today (addicted to morphine and cocaine), to writers like Ernest Hemingway, F. Scott Fitzgerald, and Dorothy Parker (all addicted to alcohol), to musicians from Billie Holiday and Eric Clapton (both addicted to heroin), to actors ranging from Judy Garland to Robin Williams (both addicted to multiple drugs) to many of today's superstars. Of course, this doesn't mean we should value neurodiversity only for the potential talent it may unleash, nor does it mean that we should ignore disastrous consequences. It does mean, however, that we should focus on people's abilities, not their disabilities, and help them find their strengths rather than stigmatize them for their weaknesses.[2]

We all learn to become who we are. And none of us starts from the same place or encounters the same cultural and social contexts in the same way. Our memories and the way our nervous systems react to them is what makes us unique. Those with addictions or other differences need to be recognized not only for their faults and frailties, but also for their talents and resources.[3]

If we must be addicted, let us be addicted to life, to simplicity, silence, kindness, equality, peace, and generosity, in other words, to self-awareness, self-understanding, and acceptance of life in all its beauty and bounty. These are enough for one lifetime, sufficient for all our needs and addictions.

2. Ibid., 283–84.
3. Ibid., 285.

# Appendix A

*Resources*

WHEN YOU FEEL TEMPTED by addictive patterns or behavior, apply the following concepts: PAY–PRAY–PLAY.

- PAY—Pay attention to the patterns in your life; be attentive to your physical, emotional, and spiritual needs; be mindful and Self-aware; pay attention to others, investing in their needs, promoting their joy and well-being; join a Bible study group or a book-reading club.

- PRAY—Ask God for patience and help with your addiction; spend time meditating, silently awaiting God's guidance, power, and transformative grace.

- PLAY—Pick up a new hobby or learn new games; Stay active by exercising regularly, and going for walks or bike rides; enjoy old friends or make new ones; consider adopting a pet from the humane society.

If you, a family member, or a friend, is stuck in addiction and has trouble letting go, consider taking one or more of the following steps:

1. If your personality disorder is severe, find a good clinical psychologist or psychiatric specialist and schedule an appointment.

2. Find a healthy church, one that is simultaneously conservative and progressive, and get involved. Beware, however, church leaders that are addicted to power and fearful of change. Learn to distinguish between religious addiction and healthy spirituality, which promotes detachment, personal growth, and authentic joy.

3. Read books on addiction, especially Maia Szalavitz's *Unbroken Brain*.

4. Go online and investigate Deepak Chopra's perspective on spirituality and success.

5. Go online and subscribe to Richard Rohr's daily meditations. Read Rohr's books *The Naked Now*, *Falling Upward*, and *The Universal Christ*.

6. Go online to learn more about the Enneagram and your personality type. Read books by Don Richard Riso and Russ Hudson, starting with *Understanding the Enneagram*.

7. Devote time daily to meditation and contemplative prayer, and read my book *In the Potter's Workshop* or any books by Thomas Keating.

Finally, meditate on two parables of Jesus found in Luke's Gospel, the parable of the Prodigal Son (15:11–32) and the parable of the Good Samaritan (10:29–37), for these parables vividly portray the aspects of addiction highlighted by our study: the cause (distorted preoccupation with self) and the solution (concern for others, particularly for people in need).

# Appendix B

*Step Four: Moral Inventory*

STEP FOUR IN TWELVE Step recovery programs involves taking moral inventory: "*Made a searching and fearless moral inventory of ourselves.*" This step—examining one's strengths and weaknesses—makes it possible to learn about ourselves, our unconscious habits and unrecognized talents, our unspoken shame, secret delights, and hidden passions. Like other steps in the program, but more so, this step involves more than a one-time examination or simple listing of virtues and vices. Rather, this step represents the beginning of a lifetime practice of honest self-examination, as Step Ten makes clear: "*Continued to take personal inventory and when we were wrong promptly admitted it.*" In essence, Step Four will help participants discover how natural desires can turn into liabilities, how good qualities can become defects, and how needs can turn into obsessions.

It is important to begin your inventory by focusing on positive traits. Most of us are accustomed to finding fault with ourselves, and we overlook our many assets. The twelve steps are means to positive change. They are not intended to increase guilt or diminish our self-image. To the contrary, they allow us to observe ourselves as we are, helping us to see through our illusions, take care of unresolved issues, make conscious choices here and now, and recognize where to turn for strength, support, and guidance. Each step plays a crucial role in restoring us to physical, emotional, and spiritual wholeness.

The following approaches to Step Four are recommended by Alcoholics Anonymous and Nicotine Anonymous.[1] Select those you find most helpful.

1. See *Twelve Steps and Twelve Traditions*, 50–54 and *Nicotine Anonymous: The Book*, 82–85.

1. Examine three dimensions of your life—sexual relations, financial security, and emotional security—by asking the following questions:

    a. When and how did my pursuit of sex relations damage other people and me? How have I reacted to frustration in sexual matters? Whom have I hurt?

    b. How have addictive behaviors influenced my financial security? What is my relationship to money and possessions? Do I use them responsibly or recklessly? Am I extravagant or miserly? If so, how and why? Do I cut corners financially?

    c. How have addictive behaviors influenced my emotional security? What roles do fear, greed, possessiveness, and pride play in my private and public life? Do I try to cover up feelings of inadequacy by bluffing, cheating, lying, or by evading responsibility? Am I truthful with others? Do I treat all people with respect?

Common symptoms of emotional insecurity are worry, anger, self-pity, and depression. To take inventory in this area, you need to consider those relationships that bring recurring trouble. To what extent have sexual relations caused anxiety, bitterness, frustration, or depression? To what extent have financial conditions aroused similar feelings? Questions such as these can help get to the root of your situation. In most cases, the fault is not yours alone. If the actions of others are part of the cause of your emotional imbalance and disharmony, what can you do about that? If you are unable to change the present state of affairs, are you willing to adjust to conditions as they are? If so, what adjustments should you make?

2. Answer the following questions:[2]

    a. How did I get started in my addiction?

    b. What was it like?

    c. Why did I decide it was time to quit?

    d. What happened?

    e. What am I like now?

---

2. These questions are headings for a detailed listing in the Nicotine Anonymous Questionnaire found in Part II of *Nicotine Anonymous: The Book*, 24–71.

3. Think about your good and bad qualities, the things about which you felt good and those about which you felt bad in the past, and how you feel about them now. Write them down and ask yourself the following questions about them.

    a. Why do I feel that way?

    b. Who else was affected by this behavior?

    c. Is this behavior part of a pattern?

    d. Am I responsible for what happened then?

    e. Am I still repeating the behavior? How?

4. Make a list of persons, institutions, principles, or events that you believe played important roles in your life. What was their influence or effect on you?

5. Examine past fears and resentments, self-loathing, or situations you stayed in long after they stopped being useful. (Many of these occurred early in life, so go back as far as you can remember, even if the details are hazy.) Anger, fear, and resentment underlie much of our addictive behavior, thwarting our ambitions, emotions, and self-esteem. Overcoming these maladies is the first step to recovering a healthy body, mind, heart, and spirit.

6. For those who dislike making lists, write a thorough and honest personal history that lets you see how you were led into addiction. What damage did addiction cause, and how has that damage influenced your behavior since?

Clear thinking and honest appraisal will help you get to the root of your situation. Taking Step Four fearlessly, free from judgment, is the first tangible evidence of your willingness to move forward.

# Bibliography

Aamouth, Doug. "Here's How Much Time People Spend Playing Video Games." No pages. Online: time.com/120476/Nielsen-video-games/.

Armstrong, Karen. *Buddha*. New York: Viking, 2001.

Benner, David G. *Spirituality and the Awakening Self: The Sacred Journey of Transformation*. Ada, MI: Brazos, 2012.

*The Big Book*. 3rd ed. New York: Alcoholics Anonymous, 1976.

Chein, Isidor, et al. *The Road to H: Narcotics, Delinquency, and Social Policy*. New York: Basic Books, 1964.

Chopra, Deepak. *The Seven Spiritual Laws of Success*. San Rafael, CA: Amber–Allen, 1994.

Delaney, Bob, and Dave Schreiber. *Surviving the Shadows*. Naperville, IL: Sourcebooks, 2011.

*Diagnostic and Statistical Manual of Mental Disorders*. 5th ed. *(DSM–5)*. Washington, D.C.: American Psychiatric, 2013.

Ellis, Albert. *Overcoming Destructive Beliefs, Feelings, and Behaviors*. Amherst, NY: Prometheus, 2001.

Erikson, E. H. *Childhood and Society*. New York: W. W. Norton, 1963.

Finley, James. *Christian Meditation; Experiencing the Presence of God*. San Francisco: HarperSanFrancisco, 2004.

Foster, Richard J. *Money, Sex & Power: The Challenge of the Disciplined Life*. San Francisco: Harper & Row, 1985.

———. *Richard J. Foster's Study Guide to The Challenge of the Disciplined Life* (Study Guide to Money, Sex & Power). San Francisco: HarperSanFrancisco, 1985.

"Gambling Addiction." No pages. Online: http://www.addictionn.com/gambling/.

Gerdy, John R. *Sports: The All-American Addiction*. Jackson, MS: University Press of Mississippi.

Hollis, James. *Finding Meaning in the Second Half of Life: How to Finally, Really Grow Up*. New York: Gotham, 2005.

*How Al-Anon Works for Families & Friends of Alcoholics*. Virginia Beach, VA: Al-Anon, 1995.

"How to Overcome Food Addiction." No pages. Online https://www.healthline.com/nutrition/how-to-overcome-food-addiction#first-steps.

Kasser, Tim. *The High Price of Materialism*. Cambridge, MA: The MIT Press, 2002.

Katerndahl, David A. "Impact of Spiritual Symptoms and Their Interactions on Health Services and Life Satisfaction." *Annals of Family Medicine* 6 (2008), 412–20. Online: www.annfammed.org/content/6/5/412.

Koblin, John. "How Much Do We Love TV? Let Us Count the Ways." No pages. Online: https://www.nytimes.com/2016/07/01/business/media/nielsen-survey-media-viewing.html.

Leary, Timothy. *Turn On, Tune In, Drop Out.* Oakland, CA: Ronin, 1965.

Lewis, C. S. *The Four Loves.* New York: Harcourt Brace, 1960.

———. *Mere Christianity.* New York: Collier, 1952.

Lindesmith, A. R. *Addiction and Opiates.* Chicago: Aldine, 1968.

Macy, Beth. *Dopesick: The Drug Company that Addicted America.* New York: Little, Brown, and Company, 2018.

May, Gerald G. *Addiction and Grace.* New York: HarperOne, 1991.

McLaren, Brian D. *Naked Spirituality.* San Francisco: HarperOne, 2011.

Musto, David. *The American Disease: Origins of Narcotic Control.* New Haven: Yale University Press, 1973.

*Narcotics Anonymous.* 6th ed. Chatsworth, CA: Narcotics Anonymous, 2008.

*Nicotine Anonymous: The Book.* 5th ed. Dallas, TX: Nicotine Anonymous, 2015.

Pariser, Eli. *The Filter Bubble: How the New Personalized Web Is Changing What We Read and How We Think.* New York: Penguin, 2011.

Peele, Stanton, and Archie Brodsky. *Love and Addiction.* New York: New American Library, 1976.

Poland, Jeffrey, and George Graham. *Addiction and Responsibility.* Cambridge, MA: The MIT Press, 2011.

Richardson, Peter Tufts. *Four Spiritualities.* Palo Alto, CA: Davies-Black, 1996.

Riso, Don Richard, and Russ Hudson. *Personality Types: Using the Enneagram for Self-Discovery.* Rev. ed. New York: Houghton Mifflin, 1996.

———. *Understanding the Enneagram.* Rev. ed. New York: Houghton Mifflin, 2000.

———. *The Wisdom of the Enneagram.* New York: Bantam, 1999.

Rohr, Richard. *The Enneagram: A Christian Perspective.* Rev. ed. New York: Crossroad, 2001.

———. *Falling Upward.* San Francisco: Jossey-Bass, 2011.

———. *The Naked Now: Learning to See as the Mystics See.* New York: Crossroad, 2004.

———. *The Universal Christ.* New York: Convergent, 2019.

Rohr, Richard, and Andreas Ebert. *Breathing Under Water: Spirituality and the Twelve Steps.* Cincinnati, OH: St. Anthony Messenger, 2011.

Rohr, Richard, and Mike Morrell. *The Divine Dance: The Trinity and Your Transformation.* New Kensington, PA: Whitaker House, 2016.

Saad, Marcelo, et al. "Are We Ready for a True Biopsychosocial-Spiritual Model? The Many Meanings of Spiritual." No pages. Online: https://www.mdpi.com/2305-6320/4/479/htm.

Sandberg, Katie M., et al. *Assessing Common Mental Health and Addiction Issues With Free-Access Instruments.* New York: Routledge, 2013.

Singer, Jefferson A. *Message in a Bottle: Stories of Men and Addiction.* New York: The Free Press, 1997.

Skinner, B. F. *Beyond Freedom and Dignity.* Middlesex: UK, Penguin, 1971.

Slater, Philip. *Wealth Addiction.* New York: E. P. Dutton, 1980.

Smith, Huston. *The World's Religions.* Rev. 2nd ed. San Francisco: HarperSanFrancisco, 1991 (1958).

Sulmasy, Daniel P. "A Biopsychosocial-Spiritual Model for the Care of Patients at the End of Life." *Gerontologist* 42:3 (2002), 24–33. Online: https://academic.oup.com/gerontologist/article/42/suppl_3/24/569213.

Szalavitz, Maia. *Unbroken Brain: A Revolutionary New Way of Understanding Addiction.* New York: St. Martin's, 2016.

*Twelve Steps and Twelve Traditions.* New York: Alcoholics Anonymous, 2013.

Vande Kappelle, Robert P., Sr. *Dark Splendor: Spiritual Fitness for the Second Half of Life.* Eugene, OR: Resource, 2015.

———. *Grace Revealed: The Message of Paul's Letter to the Romans – Then and Now.* Eugene, OR: Wipf & Stock, 2017.

———. *In the Potter's Workshop: Experiencing the Divine Presence in Everyday Life.* Eugene, OR: Wipf & Stock, 2019.

———. *Iron Sharpens Iron: A Discussion Guide for Twenty-First-Century Seekers.* Eugene, OR: Wipf & Stock, 2013.

———. *Living Graciously on Planet Earth: Faith, Hope, and Love in Biblical, Social, and Cosmic Context.* Eugene, OR: Wipf & Stock, 2016.

"Video Game Addiction." No pages. Online: https://www.addictions.com/video-games/.

Wilson, H. W. *The Digital Age.* The Reference Shelf 87:4. Amenia, NY: Grey House, 2015.

Zinberg, Norman E. *Drug, Set, and Setting.* New Haven: Yale University Press, 1984.

# Index